The Grandest Deception

The Grandest Deception

Dr. Jack Pruett

Library of Congress Control Number:		2011904786
ISBN:	Hardcover	978-1-4568-9279-1
	Softcover	978-1-4568-9278-4
	Ebook	978-1-4568-9280-7

This book was printed in the United States of America.

To order additional copies of this book, contact:

Xlibris Corporation
1-888-795-4274
www.Xlibris.com
Orders@Xlibris.com
94638

Contents

I would like to dedicate this book to Enki. He created mankind. He found a way to save us from the flood. I believe that he also found a way to help me write this book. My most sincere prayer is that he will find a way to help mankind alter the fate that the Annunaki have planned for us.

Preface

I certainly do not claim that all parts of this book are true. Some of it is speculation on my part. The overall concept is absolutely true. I have made an attempt to point out to the reader where I am speculating. Having survived almost seventy years on this planet, I feel that I have earned the right to express my opinion. I have earned the right to speculate about some things that are puzzling and bothersome to me.

I would like to express my most sincere thanks to Zecharia Sitchin. I have great respect for him and the amazing work that he has done. His books have provided many hours of pleasure and excitement for me. I must admit that when I read *The 12th Planet*, I did so primarily out of curiosity. I was intrigued with his work and soon read the rest of his books. By that time, I had been studying the Bible for many years. I never dreamed that his books would be related to the Bible in any way. I am also quite shocked at the conclusions that I have reached. It has taken me about five years of additional study of the Bible, of Sitchin's books, of the Dead Sea Scrolls, and of other materials to reach the conclusions that I have arrived at in this book. There were many times during the process that I just could not accept the idea that the Bible is not a story about God. I am absolutely convinced today that it is a story about the Annunaki. The evidence in favor of this conclusion is simply more than I can ignore.

I would also like to thank William Bramley for the outstanding research that he has done and for the wonderful book that he has written. I would recommend *The Gods of Eden* to any interested reader.

I would like to thank Queenie May with Xlibris Incorporated for inspiring me to add part two of this book; others who have been very helpful from Xlibris are Greg Fuentes and James Calonia.

I absolutely believe that the Annunaki are a race of beings who in Earth's distant past came to this planet in search of gold. They created a hybrid race, mankind, to be their slaves. They have heaped unremitting physical hardships and spiritual decay upon mankind, they consider us to be their possession, they have absolutely no regard for human life, and they still control us today. I also absolutely believe that their planet will return to the vicinity of Earth near the year of AD 3400. My sincere hope is that some who read this book will begin to seek the truth concerning these matters. I hope that after you read this book, some will cast a more suspicious eye on government and politics, on churches and religion, and on the Bible. I hope that the general public will come to understand that the Federal Reserve banking system is a monster and that it needs to be dealt with immediately. Above all, I hope that somehow this book will help humans be kinder, more understanding, and more loving toward their fellow human beings. I also wish the same for the Annunaki.

Part 1:
The Grandest
Deception

Chapter 1

WHAT IS GOING ON?

What in the heck is wrong with us? Our world is upside down. Doctors destroy our health, lawyers destroy justice, the government destroys our freedom, the mainstream media destroys information, and our religions destroy our spirituality. We are constantly at war with each other, and mankind is becoming more wicked and evil as time marches on.

I am sure that everyone who reads this book will be able to think of many examples of doctors destroying health, of lawyers perverting justice, of governments taking away our freedoms, of the mainstream media distorting information to such a degree that the truth is impossible to find, and of religions that breed hypocrisy and insane belief systems. It would be far beyond the scope of this book to explore the myriads of ways in which these things occur.

I am sixty-nine years old. I am an MD and have practiced medicine for almost forty years. After graduating from medical school, I completed a residency training program in obstetrics and gynecology. I have delivered over five thousand babies in my career. Because of this training, I know a little about genetics, embryology, artificial insemination, in vitro fertilization, and cloning. For the past twelve years, I have done general practice. During all those years, I have listened to many people tell me about their ills, their lives, their beliefs, and their opinions about numerous topics. It has been quite a trip. I grew up in a world that made sense to me. Our world today makes no sense to me. I am trying to find out what is going on, and why we are doing so many things that make no sense to me.

For instance, why has our government turned over our entire money system to a group of people over which we have absolutely no control? We have no way of holding them accountable for what they do, and we do not even know who all of them are. Why do we have a military presence in so many foreign countries when our founding fathers warned us that we should not become entangled in foreign affairs? Why do we spend so many of our hard-earned dollars on foreign aid? We have so many people in need in our own country; we also have ample evidence that most of the foreign aid does not go to people in need in those countries. The money ends up in the pockets of some dishonest politician or foreign leader. Why have we recently spent billions, or perhaps trillions, of dollars to bail out companies and banks that have done such a poor job of managing their businesses? At the same time, we have made it very difficult for small business owners to survive because of all the nonsensical federal regulations they have to endure. Why do we allow illegal aliens to come into our country? We then pay them to stay here by providing them health care and welfare checks. Why have we turned our health care system over to a government that has proven to be extremely inefficient in everything they do, except steal our money? They are very good at that. Why is our government so dishonest and so secretive about so many things? One thing that I have found out from talking to people for these many years is that no one trusts the government anymore. I could give you many other examples of things that make no sense to me, but I think you see where I am coming from.

I believe that one of the reasons our world is so upside down is that the individuals and institutions mentioned above are making decisions based on inaccurate information. One cannot make good decisions if the information upon which those decisions are based is inaccurate. For most people, certain information has been ingrained into their minds since early childhood. Information that we received as children influences what we believe as adults. If the information that has been ingrained into us since childhood is inaccurate, the decisions we make as adults are influenced by false information that oftentimes leads to bad decisions.

For example, as a child, I was taught that the Bible is the inerrant word of God. My parents, grandparents, Sunday school teachers, preachers, and most of the people I came in contact with during those years all reinforced that belief. As a child, I naturally accepted this teaching as being true without even a thought of questioning its veracity. I am sure that many of the decisions that I made were influenced to some degree by this belief. I was taught that the Bible was an instruction book about how I should live my life. When, as a young man, I began to experience some of the difficulties of life, I decided that I should read the instruction book. I read it cover to cover three or four times. I thought it very strange that a father, especially an all-knowing, loving, heavenly father, would give a child an instruction book that he could not understand. Biblical scholars, who have studied it for years, disagree about what it says.

When I later had children of my own, I realized that I had to give them very plain, simple instructions. The instructions had to be very clear if they were going to be able to follow them. Confusing them about the instructions would be of no benefit to them in any way. Nevertheless, I held on to my core beliefs concerning the Bible.

Later in my life, I began to teach Sunday school classes and eventually Bible study classes. I was teaching the same falsehoods that were taught to me as a child. After years of intense Bible study, I began to realize that there were very serious things wrong with what I believed about the Bible. There is no doubt that the good book contains great truths. It is a masterpiece of revelation, but alas, it is also a travesty of deception.

The very first sentence in the Christian Bible is absolutely loaded with deception. Genesis 1:1 says,

> In the beginning God created the heaven and
> the earth.

When I first read this sentence, I assumed that "in the beginning" meant when all things first began. We now know that the universe began about 16.5 billion years ago, but Earth is only about 4.5 billion years old. So does "in the beginning" mean when the universe was begun or when the Earth was begun? The Christian Bible says, "God created." The Hebrew Bible was written long before the Christian Bible; it should, therefore, be more accurate. The Hebrew Bible says, "The Elohim created." In Hebrew, *El* means *god* (singular) and *Elohim* means *gods* (plural): so how many gods did the creating? The Christian Bible says "the heaven and the earth" were created. The Hebrew Bible says "the hammered out bracelet and the earth" were created. The hammered-out bracelet is the asteroid belt that is located between Mars and Jupiter. What, exactly, was created?

If an all-knowing, heavenly father indeed did the creating, and if his intent was to instruct his innocent children, why would he not make clear these discrepancies? Since he owns everything, he would not run out of ink or tablets upon which to carve out the details. Since he is also eternal, there would certainly not be a time restraint. He could have made the details quite clear and had plenty of time to spare. Actually, the details concerning the formation of Earth and the asteroid belt have been described in great detail in an Akkadian text written in the old Babylonian dialect some 4,500 years ago. This text was known in antiquity by its opening words, Enuma Elish (When in the heights). It is now called the Creation Epic. Details of this can be found in the book entitled *The 12th Planet* written by Zecharia Sitchin.

In Genesis, chapter 1, verses 26–27, the Christian Bible says,

> And God said, Let us make man in our image,
> after our likeness: and let them have dominion
> over the fish of the sea, and over the fowl of the

air, and over the cattle, and over all the earth, and over every creeping thing that creepeth upon the earth. So God created man in his own image, in the image of God created he him; male and female he created them.

In English, the deception is quite obvious. Why would a singular god say, "Let us make" or "In our likeness" or "In our image"? My mother was an English teacher. She would have had a fit if I talked like that. The passages are clearer in Hebrew where Elohim (plural) is used everywhere the word *god* appears in the Christian Bible. Although I am sure that it is going to be quite difficult or impossible for many people to accept, this major deception in the Christian Bible seems to have been cleared up. The evidence, at least, is very difficult to deny. It appears that human beings (*Homo sapiens*) were not created by a single god or by multiple gods. Mankind, *Homo sapiens*, was created by ancient astronauts from another planet.

They created us to serve as a slave race to do the work they needed done here on planet Earth. They created us in such a way that about 20 percent of our DNA came from a hominid that they called ape-woman. And about 80 percent of our DNA came from a male of their species. Their "Adam" was created about 290,000 years ago. The details of how they created us were described in detail in ancient Sumerian texts. They can also be found in Sitchin's *The 12th Planet*. The evidence for the truth concerning our creation is very difficult to dispute. For anyone who is interested in verifying for him/herself these facts, I would recommend beginning with Sitchin's the Earth Chronicles, a series of books that he wrote after exhaustive research and study of the ancient texts.

The Christian Bible in Genesis 6:4 states,

> There were giants in the earth in those days; and also after that, when the sons of God came in unto the daughters of men, and they bare children to them, the same became mighty men which were of old, men of renown.

In the Hebrew Bible, the verses read,

> The Nefilim were upon the earth, in those days and thereafter too, when the sons of the gods cohabited with the daughters of the Adam, and they bore children unto them. They were the mighty ones of Eternity—the people of the shem.

In Hebrew, *Nefilim* means "those who were cast down," and *shem* means "rocket ship." The theological implications may be difficult for some; nevertheless, the original meaning of these verses is that the sons of the gods who came to earth from the heavens were the Nefilim. And the Nefilim were the people of the rocket ships, i.e., ancient astronauts.

Who were these ancient astronauts? Were they gods? The answer to the first question is that the ancient Sumerian texts call them *Annunaki*. Sitchin has made it quite clear in his great works that the Annunaki were not gods. They fought, fucked, and died. None of those are considered to be godly behavior. The Annunaki are a race of beings who are far more advanced technologically and culturally than we are. They indeed created us in their image and likeness. We are therefore much like them. However, we are still far less advanced and far less intelligent than they are.

As painful as it may be, when one reads the Bible, they would have a much clearer understanding of the truth if Annunaki, Nefilim, or ancient astronauts was substituted everywhere *God* or *Elohim* occurs. I have believed all my life that there is a Supreme Being, God. I still believe that there is. The Annunaki are not gods even though the Bible calls them *God* or *Elohim*. In fact, one of the psalmists may have realized that the Annunaki were not gods and written a psalm to that effect, Psalm 82:

> God standeth in the congregation of the mighty;
> he judgeth among the gods [Elohim]. How long

will ye judge unjustly, and accept the persons of the wicked? Selah.

Defend the poor and fatherless: do justice to the afflicted and needy.

Deliver the poor and needy: rid them out of the hand of the wicked.

They know not, neither will they understand; they walk on in darkness: all the foundations of the earth are out of course. I have said, Ye are gods [Elohim]; and all of you are children of the most High.

But ye shall die like men, and fall like one of the princes. Arise, O God, judge the earth: for thou shalt inherit all nations.

A man named Asaph wrote that psalm, as well as eleven more. He was appointed minister of music in the temple during the time of King David. I believe that this psalm is addressing the Annunaki when it says, "But ye shall die like men." What do you think is meant by "all the foundations of the earth are out of course?" Perhaps you will have a better understanding of what that means by the time you finish this book.

Interestingly, in one of Sitchin's books entitled *Divine Encounters,* he states that the ancient tablets say that the Annunaki believe that the Supreme Being created them. The Bible is not a story about God or the Supreme Being. The Bible is a story about the Annunaki. That, my friends, is *the grandest deception* and has far-reaching implications.

Chapter 2

THE ANNUNAKI

Zecharia Sitchin, an internationally acclaimed author and researcher, has written a series of books called the Earth Chronicles, which go into great detail about the Annunaki, their arrival on Earth, and their adventures on this planet. He has also written three more books concerning these beings. The information upon which Sitchin based his works was derived from many sources. The primary source, however, was ancient tablets found in Iraq and surrounding areas. The tablets were found in the excavations from the lands mentioned in the Bible; many of the tablets were over seven thousand years old. They had been written by people who are known as Sumerians. Sumer was the first city to be civilized after the flood. This was the land of the Garden of Eden. Sitchin proves beyond any reasonable doubt that the gods who dwelt in the Garden of Eden, who created mankind, and who wrote the ancient Sumerian tablets were the Annunaki. The Sumerian tablets identify the Annunaki as "those who from heaven to Earth came." They came to Earth from a planet called Nibiru.

The creation epic, mentioned earlier in this book, is a long, sophisticated cosmogony. It was written on seven tablets (seven days of creation) and explains in great detail how Earth, moon, and asteroid belt were formed. A moon of a planet called Nibiru collided with another planet called Tiamat; this created a fissure in Tiamat.

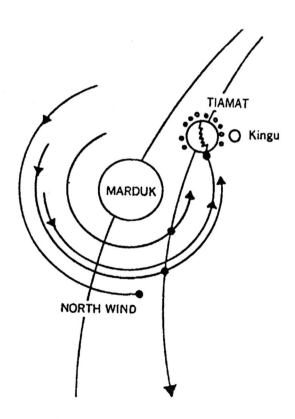

After orbiting the sun, Nibiru hit Tiamat. This split Tiamat in half. One-half became Earth; the other half became the asteroid belt. A moon of Tiamat became the moon of Earth. And the planet of Nibiru was captured into a long elliptical orbit around our sun. Each orbit of Nibiru takes about 3,600 years to complete.

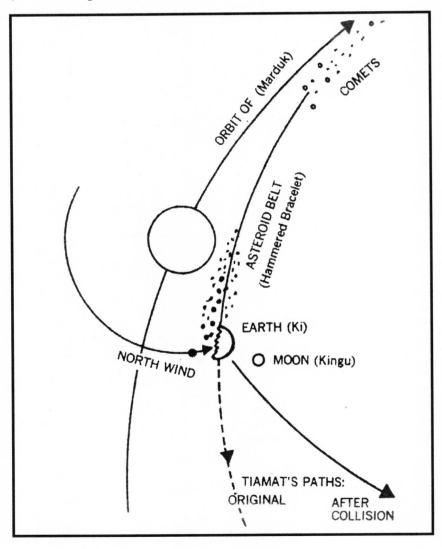

After orbiting the sun, Nibiru (twelfth planet/ Marduk) strikes Tiamat. The Earth, moon, and asteroid belt are formed.

The orbital path of Nibiru runs in a clockwise direction. The rest of the celestial bodies in our solar system orbit in a counterclockwise direction.

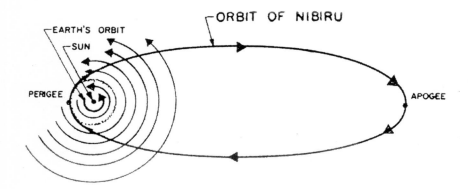

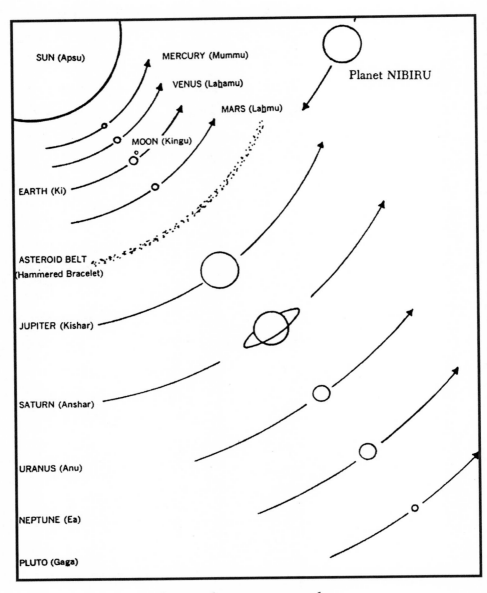

Our solar system today.

How, unless they were eyewitnesses to these events that occurred 4.5 billion years ago, could the Annunaki have known such intricate details concerning the creation of Earth, moon, and asteroid belt? If they were eyewitnesses, they have had to exist as a race on Nibiru for over 4.5 billion years. Imagine, if you can, what the human race will be like if we survive for 4.5 billion years. Our best science today confirms the accuracy of the details of the creation of Earth, moon, and asteroid belt as described in the ancient tablets.

If an Annunaki ages one year each time Nibiru completes an orbit around the sun, a human would age 3,600 years in the same time span. The Annunaki should have much longer life spans than humans since their technology and medical capabilities are far advanced compared to ours. But if we just use the ratio of 1/3,600, a one-hundred-year-old human would be equivalent to a 360,000-year-old Annunaki. Enki, the Annunaki's greatest scientist, found that ape-woman had a very short life span. Humans had a longer life span; it was still quite short compared to the Annunaki. Children of the Annunaki who were born on planet Earth had longer life spans than humans but significantly shorter life spans than their parents. Mission control, we have a problem.

Since humans have such a short life span, it is easy to understand how we would think that the Annunaki were gods. An Annunaki would not appear to have aged at all during the entire life of the human. The Annunaki also had rocket ships, flying machines, and other technologies that would seem far advanced to us, even today. Certainly, the humans described in the book of Genesis in the Bible would think that the Annunaki were gods. The first eight chapters of the book of Genesis cover a period of at least 4.5 billion years. The Annunaki have been here for at least 445,000 of those years. They wrote the original accounts of the stories that were later edited, condensed, altered, and eventually turned into the Bible. I believe that these edited versions have been continually altered over the years in order to suit the agenda of the Annunaki.

When we consider the technology available to the Annunaki, the miracles described in the Bible are not so miraculous. Likewise, when we consider the longevity of the Annunaki, the prophecies are not so prophetic. For instance, if someone told someone to prophesize that an event was going to occur, and if that event did occur six hundred years later, to our human minds that does seem that only God could have foreknown of that event. However, six hundred years is equivalent to two months in the lifetime of an Annunaki. The Annunaki were great planners and organizers. They had specific goals to meet, and the Annunaki were utilizing humans to help them achieve their goals. Viewed in this light, biblical prophecy is not as divinely inspired as it was once thought to be.

The great Annunaki are certainly far ahead of us. They possessed technologies over four hundred thousand years ago that we haven't even dreamed of yet. Some of those technologies concerned genetics, health care, longevity, and even death and resurrection from the dead. In spite of such advances, the Annunaki have always been preoccupied with the problem of their life span. In order to maintain their longer cycles on the quick-paced Earth, the astronauts consumed a "Food of Life" and "Water of Life," which were provided from the home planet. We do not know whether the Annunaki ever solved the longevity problem of their descendents who were born on Earth. We do know that they refused to share their knowledge concerning longevity with mankind.

The Annunaki originally came to Earth about 450,000 years ago. An Annunaki ruler named Alalu had been deposed by a more powerful ruler named Anu. Anu had become the ruler of Nibiru through a coup d'état that forced Alalu to flee the planet. Alalu found refuge on planet Earth and noted that gold was present here. The inhabitants of Nibiru were in search of gold. Sitchin suggested that they might need gold to repair their atmosphere, which was deteriorating. He proposed the possibility that dispersing flakes of gold into their atmosphere might correct the problem. Alalu apparently sent word back to Nibiru that he had found gold; perhaps this was done in order to gain favor with Anu. But as we shall see, the Annunaki are not quick to forgive and forget.

Enki, a son of Anu, was sent to Earth, with about fifty others, to search for the gold. This was approximately 445,000 years ago. Enki and his group spent about 28,800 years cleaning up the place, building homes, and searching for gold. They had arrived on Earth in the midst of an ice age, and conditions were harsh. But the decision was made to move forward with the project. Another son of Anu, Enlil, who was actually in charge of the project all along, was then sent to planet Earth with other Annunaki reinforcements. The total number of Annunaki present on Earth at that time was about three hundred.

The two sons of Anu were actually half brothers; they had different mothers. Enki was the firstborn son of Anu; however, his mother was not the official wife of Anu. Enlil was the second-born son. His mother was Antu, who was also a half sister of her husband, Anu. The maternal families of these two boys had been engaged in a family dispute back on Nibiru for some time over which son would succeed Anu as king and receive his inheritance. The succession rule was that the firstborn son is next in succession. However, the rule also stated that the king could marry a half sister if they had different mothers, and if a son was produced from that union (even if not firstborn), he becomes the legal heir and next king.

This succession rule seems to be based on very sophisticated genetics. I believe that our scientists should investigate this matter further. Why do the Annunaki place such importance on a male offspring born to a half brother and half sister with different mothers? If our scientists can answer that question, I believe that we would obtain knowledge that would be very beneficial to mankind. In order to understand the story of the Annunaki, and thus the Bible, one must understand this rule of succession. Please keep this rule in mind as you read this book.

The disputes between these half brothers did not end just because they came to Earth and got involved in a project together. Their rivalries included matters of the heart (especially one concerning a half sister), as well as disputes over many other things. Eventually Anu came to Earth to try to settle the dispute between the two half brothers; he offered to stay on Earth and let one of the half brothers assume the regency on Nibiru. The ancient texts tell us that lots were cast to determine who would rule where. The result was that Anu returned as king of Nibiru, Enlil became "Lord of the Command" and was in overall charge of the Earth project, and Enki was put in charge of the AB.ZU. He was given dominion over the seas and waters. I cannot imagine that God would do business in that manner.

The word in Akkadian for *AB.ZU* is *apsu*; the English word for abyss comes from the Akkadian *apsu*. The Bible seems to equate the abyss with the bottomless pit, Hades, or hell. The abyss is located underground, and the Bible in 2 Peter 2:4 says,

> For if God spared not the angels that sinned, but cast them down to hell, and delivered them into chains of darkness, to be reserved unto judgment.

Sitchin believes that the AB.ZU refers to the southern hemisphere of Earth. I believe that it also includes the underground facilities of the Annunaki.

We know that the Annunaki committed crimes; they appointed a sheriff. There are also stories in the ancient tablets about various Annunaki expressing great fear over the possibility that they would be imprisoned in this underground locale. I believe that at least some portion of the AB.ZU was used as an underground jail or prison to house Annunaki who committed crimes. Humans who committed crimes were usually just killed. As I will show later, for an Annunaki to be held in prison for several hundred thousand years awaiting trial (judgment) would be no big deal.

I agree with Sitchin that we have misinterpreted the AB.ZU, abyss, and hell to mean the "world of the dead." I question, however, whether Sitchin is correct when he concludes that Enki's domain referred only to Africa or the southern hemisphere of Earth. Enki was, indeed, in charge of the gold mining operation in Africa. But the ancient texts describe travel by living beings back and forth from the upper world to the lower world on many occasions, and in some instances the lower world is subterranean. Is it possible that the ancient texts should be taken literally and that the AB.ZU includes the abyss or bottomless pit that is mentioned in the Bible? Was Enlil put in charge of developing the aboveground operations and Enki put in charge of developing the underground operations? Enlil was deemed Lord Earth and Enki, Lord Water. Is it possible that Enki, with all his expertise, was assigned the job of developing underground accommodations for the Annunaki, and could these underground accommodations have entranceways from an ocean or some underwater location? There is some evidence that there is a natural entranceway to the underworld at the South Pole. There is also evidence in the ancient tablets that Enki was given the epithet of Lucifer. Lucifer means carrier or bearer of light. Could Enki have gotten this epithet because he brought light to the underground? Could this epithet for Satan, the devil, and Enki mean that they are one and the same person? I believe that they are.

There is no doubt that the Annunaki were master builders. There are numerous examples of their master craftsmanship aboveground. There are places where huge stones, weighing hundreds of thousands of tons, have been precisely quarried, moved over hundreds of miles, and placed in very precise ways. Some examples of such achievements are Solomon's Temple in Jerusalem, the Aztec temples in Mexico, the Maya temples in the Yucatan, the Inca temples in Peru, Stonehenge in England, and of course, the pyramids in Egypt, as well as others in various parts of the world. And what about the Nazca Lines in Peru? Only the great Annunaki could have built such structures.

With the advanced technology that they obviously possessed in order to build such amazing structures aboveground, it is not much of a stretch to believe that they could also build amazing cities underground. In fact, someone has. We have found huge underground excavations in numerous places around the world. Some of these underground excavations could comfortably support fifty thousand inhabitants. Some of them contain as many as eight stories of dwellings, and they are ventilated so perfectly that even on the deepest floor the air is very fresh. Some of them contain huge sarcophagi, weighing as much as sixty tons. The huge sarcophagi have been placed in the niches of the caverns. Not unexpectedly, some of these are located beneath some of our largest cities (Athens, Paris, Los Angeles). Who could have built such structures and had a need for such sarcophagi but the Annunaki?

Even though the half brothers were separated by great distances, the feuding did not let up. They were constantly at each other's throat. Their descendents would become involved in the family feud. Their hybrid creation would also become involved. An event of great importance in the Bible, the flood, led to one of the disputes between Enki and Enlil. The edited/altered version of the flood is found in chapters 6–9 of Genesis in the Old Testament. The dispute involved Noah and the saving of mankind.

After humans had been given the ability to procreate, they multiplied fairly rapidly. Although they were working in the gold mines as well as performing other slave duties, Enlil became disgruntled with them. He felt that they had become too noisy and boisterous; he wanted to rid Earth of them. At times, my children and grandchildren have been that way as well.

The Annunaki knew that a great natural disaster was going to occur, causing a huge flood. Enlil viewed this as a means to get rid of the bothersome humans. All the Annunaki had pledged an oath to not save the humans from the disaster. Enki, however, knew that there was a very special human on Earth. This human possessed very special genetic traits. Enki wanted to save this man. In spite of his vow, he found a way to inform this person (the biblical Noah) of the impending disaster. The Sumerian name for Noah was Ziusudra. Enki gave Ziusudra specific instructions about how to build a submersible boat, a submarine. He also provided Ziusudra a navigator who had instructions to guide the submarine toward Mount

Ararat. Ziusudra was further advised to take as many seeds from various plants on board as he could. He was also given eggs and sperm from many animals to take on board; these would be used to reproduce those animals after the waters had subsided. Please remember that these tablets were written some seven thousand years ago. The Annunaki lifted off from Earth in their rocket ships and, while in Earth orbit, viewed the catastrophe from above. When the Annunaki returned to Earth, Enlil was infuriated to find that some humans had survived. He realized that Enki had broken his vow. This only heightened the animosity between the half brothers.

The flood occurred about thirteen thousand years ago. The details of the Annunaki version of the story can be found in Sitchin's, *The 12th Planet*. I quote from him: "These nagging doubts of the story's veracity disperse, however, when we realize that the biblical account is an edited version of the original Sumerian account. As in the other instances, the monotheistic Bible has compressed into one deity the roles played by several gods who were not always in accord."

The feud between the two half brothers had begun on Nibiru, had continued for at least 432,000 years until the flood occurred, and would only intensify after the flood. In book three of the Earth Chronicles entitled *The Wars of Gods and Men*, Sitchin does an amazing job of describing this family feud. He describes the wars that were fought between the half brothers and their descendents; these wars began soon after Enlil's arrival on Earth. Alalu was killed in the process. The wars continued almost nonstop, even after the flood. They eventually resulted in nuclear weapons being used to destroy the spaceport in the Sinai Peninsula in 2024 BCE. Sitchin also does an amazing job of describing how mankind, the hybrid slaves of the Annunaki, were coerced, conned, and manipulated by both sides to participate in these wars. Even the use of nuclear weapons did not bring a conclusion to the family feud. The use of nuclear weapons just resulted in the Annunaki delegating more responsibility to the slaves to continue the battles while the Annunaki took a less-active role. For the last four thousand years, mankind has continued to be coerced, conned, and manipulated into continuing the struggle.

In Sitchin's last book entitled *The End of Days*, he presents convincing evidence that there was a mass exodus of Annunaki from about 610–560 BCE. Nibiru caused the flood in approximately 11,000 BCE when it passed near Earth in its orbit. It returns every 3,600 years. The next passage of Nibiru occurred around 7400 BCE; this was a time of relative peace on Earth when the Neolithic period began and the demigods ruled over Egypt. The next passage was around 3800 BCE; Sumer was founded, civilization exploded upon Earth with many new advances, and Anu came to Earth for a visit. The next

passage was around 200 BCE; preparations for the birth
of Jesus were being made. So what did the Annunaki do
from 560 BCE until 200 BCE while awaiting the return of
Nibiru so that they could go home?

They had created a relay station on Mars that was used
to shuttle things back and forth between Earth, Mars, and
Nibiru. I believe that they went to the relay station on Mars
and slept. The Bible says in numerous places that a day for
them is like a thousand years for us. We sleep about eight
hours a day (one-third of our day). We are created in their
image and likeness; I would assume that they also sleep
about one-third of their day. So a 333-year sleep seems quite
reasonable. It is also interesting that there seems to be a
lot of times in the ancient texts where one or another of
the Annunaki is not heard from for three to four hundred
years at a time. Whatever the case may be, I am sure that
they wanted to be well rested for all the festivities that would
surely take place on Nibiru when they returned.

The Annunaki had amassed a tremendous amount
of gold by that time; I believe that a massive amount
of gold departed with them on those flights. The Bible
describes the huge amounts of gold that King Solomon
had amassed. Could the Annunaki have put him on the
throne in order to do just that? (We now know why King
Solomon was so wise.) And could the gold that King
Solomon accumulated have departed with them at that
time? It disappeared, and no one has found it for over

2,500 years. We also have stories about huge amounts of gold that had been accumulated in Mexico by the Aztecs, in Peru by the Incas, in Egypt by the pharaohs, and in other places that have never been found. How could that much gold just disappear? I doubt that it did. I suspect that it went to Nibiru.

Still, this was 560 BCE. There was a lot of gold left on planet Earth. The first generation Annunaki had been here for over 440,000 years. They had endured much, they had invested huge amounts of resources into the project, and they had achieved great things. It was time for them to go home; however, I do not believe for one minute that they just abandoned a project that they had put so much into.

Apparently, they somewhat have a sense of humor. Sitchin, in his last book entitled *The End of Days*, has presented convincing evidence that the Nazca Lines were made by the exhausts from the rockets that the Annunaki left in. On their way out, they also had a little fun by doodling into the earth the huge animals at Nazca that can only be seen from space. Leaving from Nazca had become necessary because the spaceport in the Sinai Peninsula had been destroyed. This group had been involved in wars over the succession rights to the throne of Nibiru for almost the entire time that they had been on Earth. I suspect that the old-timers were happy to get out of here and go home. It was time for the kids and grandkids to take over.

The underground accommodations would have easily been completed by that time. The longevity problem might still exist on the surface. The Annunaki may have disappeared from the surface of Earth. I strongly believe that they are still in total control, probably from underground facilities of some sort.

Enki wanted to go home with the rest of the group; I have reason to believe that Enki realized that once the flights reached Nibiru, the succession rule would be upheld. Enlil would be crowned king and succeed Anu as the next ruler of Nibiru. Enki and his supporters (I will call them Enkiites) may have attacked the craft carrying Enlil and his supporters (I will call them Enlilites). The craft carrying the Enkiites may have been damaged or who knows what might have happened, but the Enkiites were forced to return to Earth. The edited/altered version of this "Star Wars" incident may appear in the Bible in Revelation 12:7–9:

> And there was war in heaven. Michael and his angels fought against the dragon, and the dragon and his angels fought back. But he was not strong enough, and they lost their place in heaven. The great dragon was hurled down—that ancient serpent called the devil, or Satan, who leads the whole world astray. He was hurled to the earth, and his angels with him.

So it seems that Enlil went home, but Enki and his entourage remained on Earth. Enki is still here today (living underground); he is running the world. He is amassing more gold and seeing to it that the Annunaki agenda is carried out.

Chapter 3

THE HYBRIDS

The Adam was created about 290,000 years ago. The first hybrid (first Adam) was sterile. We obtain the same result (a sterile hybrid—a mule) when we cross a horse and a donkey. The Annunaki had become tired of mining the gold. They wanted a slave to do the work. The first slave had been produced. They needed more. Fourteen Annunaki females volunteered to be birth goddesses. The embryos were prepared, they were implanted into the birth goddesses, and the process of making slaves had begun. Seven males and seven females were produced. One of the ancient texts had this to say about those first, sterile slaves:

When Mankind was first created
They knew not the eating of bread,
knew not the wearing of garments.
They ate plants with their mouths, like sheep;
They drank water from the ditch.

The Annunaki had found a way to make slaves. The normal gestational age for humans (the first day of the last menstrual cycle until the expected date of delivery) is 280 days. If the normal gestational age for Annunaki females is the same as it is for humans, they were only producing 14 slaves every nine months at best. If we use the same ratio of 3600/1 that we used for life span, a normal gestational age for an Annunaki female would be 280 × 3600 = 1,008,000 days. That number divided by 365 days per year would be 2,761 years. They may have been producing only fourteen slaves every 2,761 years; if so, it was going to take the Annunaki a while to create a productive workforce.

I do not know what the gestational age for the Annunaki is, but because of their longer life spans, I would think that their gestational age is also much longer. There is other evidence to support this hypothesis. The Annunaki had been on Earth for about 155,000 years before the first Adam was created. They have remained here for about

290,000 more years; yet the size of their families is no greater than that of an average human family. Even if they were producing fourteen slaves per year, a better solution had to be found; indeed it was. The Bible contains the edited/altered version of the story. Some scholars entitle the story "The Temptation," and it is found in the third chapter of Genesis.

Before I discuss the temptation, I would like to help out the archaeologists a little bit. It was commonly accepted for years, especially among archaeologists, that as excavations of civilizations went deeper, each civilization would become more primitive. When the olden cities of Genesis were excavated, just the opposite occurred. As the archaeologists went deeper, each civilization became more advanced. To my knowledge, the archaeologists have never given a proper explanation for why they found this strange phenomenon. The answer is quite simple. The ancient texts say that the most Annunaki who were ever on Earth at one time was six hundred. From time to time, some of the Annunaki would return to Nibiru; others would take their place here on Earth. But the maximum number of astronauts on Earth at any one time was six hundred. The olden cities of Genesis were founded by the Annunaki; these cities were highly advanced. With time, humans were produced and eventually allowed to dwell within the cities; that city was less advanced than the one that contained only Annunaki. The Annunaki were producing additional Annunaki very slowly compared to the humans. The influence of the Annunaki was becoming diluted with each succeeding civilization. The sheer numbers of humans that were being produced so rapidly was simply destroying the Gardens of Eden.

The story of the temptation in Genesis says that God had instructed Adam and Eve not to eat from the tree in the middle of the garden. This tree has been called the Tree of Knowledge. In the Bible story, a serpent tempted Eve to eat from the tree. In some of the ancient tablets, the Annunaki were also known as the serpent people. Enki is referred to as that ancient serpent or dragon in many ancient texts. He and his half sister were the ones who were primarily responsible for creating mankind. The half sister's name was Ninharsag. She was also the chief medical officer for the Annunaki. The symbol for the American Medical Association is still two intertwined serpents encircling a pole. I believe that the intertwined serpents represent the strands of DNA, and the pole represents the tree of life. A more hidden message, if one has some knowledge of the ancient texts, is that the serpent people were the creators of mankind.

The Bible says that Adam and Eve were expelled from the Garden of Eden because they disobeyed God and ate from the tree. We are also told that all human beings must die because of this act of disobedience by one man. We were going to die anyway; even the Annunaki die.

The true story, rather than the one of deception that we get from the Bible, is that Enki and Ninharsag did some genetic engineering and produced an Adam and Eve who could reproduce. This was done so that the slaves could be produced at a faster rate. The now fertile hybrids were expelled from the Garden of Eden because they began to copulate and reproduce like rabbits, or so it seemed to the Annunaki. The Annunaki certainly did not want to have to put up with all that. Some of these hybrids gained their freedom when mankind was expelled from the Garden of Eden. Mankind began to roam the Earth.

Mankind was also told that we have a sinful nature and that we are all sinners because we were produced from a sinful act, sex. There are all kinds of admonitions about sex in the Bible. These admonitions are primarily concerned with whom we should not have sex with. These admonitions have nothing to do with sin; they are for genetic purposes. I will explain that in more detail later in this book. These admonitions can be found in Leviticus chapter 18. We were created in the image and likeness of the Annunaki. They are very sinful. We are certainly sinful, but our sinful nature has nothing to do with the fact that we were produced from a sexual act. The deception created about original sin and mankind's sinful nature does, however, have a lot to do with the Annunaki being able to control us. They have used such tactics to help them manipulate and coerce us into doing their bidding for thousands of years. Unfortunately, the same nonsense is still working today.

In chapter 5 of Genesis, we are given the life spans of Adam and the other patriarchs through Lamech, the father of Noah. The Bible tells us that Adam lived 930 years, Seth lived 912 years, Enosh lived 905 years, and after a few more, the father of Noah, Lamech, lived 777 years. Sitchin presents convincing evidence in the Earth Chronicles that each of these ages should be multiplied by a factor of 60 in order to obtain the true life spans of the patriarchs who lived prior to the flood. The true life span of Adam should be 55,800 years, Seth should be 54,720 years, Enosh should be 54,300 years, etc. The inerrant word of God appears to be errant by a factor of 60 in these cases. If one then takes the ages of these patriarchs when they had the sons described above, i.e., 130 for Adam, 105 for Seth, 90 for Enosh, etc., plus 600 years for the age that Noah was when the flood occurred, one arrives at a total of 1,656 years. Then 60 × 1,656 plus 13,000 years (for the number of years ago that the flood occurred) one arrives at 112,360 years ago when Adam the hybrid who could reproduce was created.

Adam the sterile hybrid was created about 290,000 years ago. The first Adam and the other slaves who were produced by the birth goddesses had been used in the gold mines as well as the Garden of Eden for about 290,000—12,360 = 177,640 years. The number of years that mankind has existed on Earth in our present form, *Homo sapiens,* should then be 112,360 years. I will also explain this in greater detail later. For now, let me just say that these numbers are very compatible with what we know about the beginnings of mankind.

After the flood, Shem (one of Noah's sons) lived 600 years. Several generations later, Terah, the father of Abraham, lived 205 years. I think that it is safe to say that since the Annunaki life spans were shortened when exposed to the quick-paced cycles on Earth compared to Nibiru, the hybrids they created were likewise affected. I believe that it is also safe to say that Annunaki life spans would continue to shorten if they remained on Earth.

How did the Annunaki develop such long life spans to start with? Part of the answer, at least, may be that they evolved on a planet that traveled through the deep reaches of space where they were not exposed to sunlight except for very limited times. Then, how could one survive on such a planet? The temperatures on the surface of such a planet would be extremely cold. They might have evolved underground where they would have had heat generated from the interior of the planet. If so, they would be comfortable living underground and would certainly know how to do it. They might also just prefer to live underground. The Annunaki must have known, from the onset of the project, that they would need underground accommodations on this hostile planet. If so, they put Enki in charge of developing such accommodations.

Did they solve their longevity problem on planet Earth by going underground? Who knows? But there is evidence to suggest that the hypothesis concerning underground evolution may well be true. There is an extremely interesting passage in the book of Enoch that might be a clue. This passage is also quoted in the Earth Chronicles by Sitchin in book II, which is entitled *The Stairway to Heaven.* The passage concerns the birth of Noah and states,

> His body was white as snow and red as the blooming of a rose, and the hair of his head and his long locks were white as wool, and his eyes were beautiful. And when he opened his eyes, he lighted up the whole house like the sun, and the whole house was very bright. And thereupon he arose in the hands of the midwife, opened his mouth, and conversed with the Lord of Righteousness.

This is such a fascinating passage, but I must digress before getting back to the subject at hand.

The book of Enoch is one of the ancient books. Much of it had been lost to us. When the Dead Sea Scrolls were found, fragments of the book of Enoch were among the finds. This book, written by one of the patriarchs, was undoubtedly very revered in ancient times. The Bible says in Genesis 5:21–24:

> And Enoch had lived sixty and five years, and begat Methuselah: And Enoch walked with god after he begat Methuselah three hundred years, and begat sons and daughters: And all the days of Enoch were three hundred sixty and five years: And Enoch walked with God: and he was not; for God took him.

I had always been taught that God had transformed Enoch and taken him to heaven; however, the translations of the ancient Sumerian tablets make it clear that Enoch was placed in the Garden of Eden by the Annunaki and given other duties. There is some evidence found in the Dead Sea Scrolls that one of Enoch's duties could have been to write scripture that was going to be given to humans. The question that arises is how could a book that was written by a man who walked with God for three hundred years not become part of our Bible? I believe that the book of Enoch was so inclusive that it

THE GRANDEST DECEPTION 55

contained information that the Annunaki did not want mankind to have.

Lamech was Noah's father, according to the Bible. Needless to say, he was quite shocked when he saw Noah. Lamech immediately went to his father, Methuselah, and told him,

> I have begotten a strange son, diverse from and unlike Man, and resembling the sons of the God of Heaven; and his nature is different, and he is not like us—And it seems to me that he is not sprung from me but from the angels.

The Sumerian texts say that Noah (Ziusudra) was highly favored by Enki. Noah certainly possessed some amazing genetic traits. Enki chose to reveal the oncoming flood to him in spite of the fact that he had taken a vow with the other Annunaki not to do so. What was so special about Noah?

Lamech also said to Methuselah,

> I petition thee and implore thee that thou mayest go to Enoch thy father, and learn from him the truth, for his dwelling place is amongst the angels.

Methuselah agreed to go to Enoch and reported the unusual child. Enoch made some inquiries; he reported

back to Methuselah that the boy was indeed the son of
Lamech. Enoch told Methuselah that Noah's unusual
countenance was a sign of things to come. Enoch said
to Methuselah, "There shall be a Deluge and great
destruction for one year," and the only son, who is to
be named Noah (Respite), and his family shall be saved.
These future things, Enoch told Methuselah, "I have read
in the heavenly tablets."

Furthermore, the book of Enoch states that Noah
immediately arose, following his birth, and spoke with the
Lord of Righteousness. Could the Lord of Righteousness
who Noah spoke with have been Enki? If so, Enki must
have known that this was going to be a very special birth.
Why else would he have taken the time to attend the birth
of a mere slave (human)? Noah (Ziusudra), of course, was
not a mere slave. There were some very special genetics
involved in this whole affair.

Another scroll fragment was found in the Dead Sea
Scrolls at Qumran that dealt with the unusual birth of
Noah. It states,

> Behold, I thought in my heart that the conception
> was from one of The Nefilim, one of the Holy
> Ones, and (that the child really belonged) to the
> Nefilim. And my heart was changed within me
> because of the child. Then I, Lamech, hastened
> and went to Bath-Enosh (my) wife, and I said

to her: [I want you to take an oath] by the Most
High, by the Lord Supreme, the King of all the
worlds, the ruler of the Sons of Heaven, that you
will tell me the truth whether.

Noah must certainly have been different. His favored
status was not because of his righteousness as the Bible
states; it was because of his very special genetic makeup.

Well, back to the topics of the Annunaki possibly
evolving underground and possibly living underground
now. It seems to me that a child who is snow white with
hair as white as wool would fit underground evolution
of a race. Eyes that lit up the whole house when opened
would also be quite compatible with a hypothesis of
underground evolution where it would be quite dark.
Could this be where our gene for albinism came from?
I cannot imagine how a gene for albinism could have
ever evolved on a planet like ours where the surface
inhabitants were constantly exposed to sunlight. And
Noah looked like the Annunaki. Could Enki have been
the father of Noah?

By the way, Charles Darwin was correct. The Annunaki
simply interrupted the process of evolution before it ever
got to *Homo sapiens*. Of course, the evolutionary process
on this planet may have never gotten to *Homo sapiens*. Who
knows what ape-woman and her relatives may have evolved
into had the Annunaki not interrupted the process? Even

though the Annunaki are like us, i.e., some of them are real scoundrels, we humans do owe them our very existence. Without them, we would not be here today.

When one ponders about the possibility of an entire race of beings evolving underground, there are certainly some distinct advantages for such. They would not be exposed to the many destructive forces that occur on the surface such as wind, rain, lightning, sunlight, etc. The entire process might move along much more rapidly underground. Perhaps that partly explains how evolution on Nibiru got so far ahead of the process on Earth. I will have more to say about the underground later.

Chapter 4

MORE DECEPTION

In order for the Annunaki to carry out a project as massive as theirs was on planet Earth, they had to be tremendously good organizers and planners. Could the original pioneers to Earth have always planned to return to Nibiru someday? One would certainly think so. But could they have also been clever enough to leave progeny behind to take over the project? Could their sexual escapades with the daughters of men been more than just frolic? Could they have actually planned all along for these descendents to oversee the project and run the world?

I can recall that when I was a young man, reading the Bible for about the third time, it seemed as though it was like a play that had been written by God. The characters in the play were just acting out the roles that had been given them. Do you recall that Enoch told Methuselah that he had read in the heavenly tablets about the flood and about Noah? Could it be that Enoch was given the job of writing the script for mankind? Can the Annunaki control us so well that they can write scripts for our lives and then see to it that we play out that script? At times, it certainly seems so. I do not think that they control everyone; the slaves have become too numerous. I am not going to describe in this book all the ways that they kill millions of us to reduce the numbers, but I do believe that they choose some people to play the leading roles for their play. They then control those people in some way so that the Annunaki agenda is fulfilled. Mind control is a fascinating topic but one that is far beyond the scope of this book.

The Annunaki are making quite an effort to obtain as much information as possible on each human so that they can control more of us. I believe that they also maintain detailed records of our genetic makeup. Most people would be absolutely shocked if they knew how much information about them is contained just on the strip on their driver's license. They are convincing parents to put chips in their children so that they can be found in case they get lost or kidnapped; do not believe for one second that that is the reason that they want the chip in your kid. They are convincing people to have their medical records put in a chip and placed under their skin. They have had laws passed that require that all medical records will have to conform to certain formats. Those records will have to be created electronically. Any clever computer hacker will be able to access all your medical records. The Annunaki will certainly have access to them. There has been a big effort of late to require all Americans to have a federal ID number. If that ever passes, everything that is known about you will be encoded into your federal ID card. Of course, all of us are going to have to have a chip before long if we want to be able to buy or sell anything, according to Revelation 13:16–17:

> And he causeth all, both small and great, rich and poor, free and bond, to receive a mark in their right hand, or in their foreheads: And that no man might buy or sell, save he that had the mark, or the name of the beast, or the number of his name.

That chip will also contain every detail of your life. It would be quite interesting to have one of those chips. It will not only contain information about you, it will also contain your family tree back to one of the seven Eves. The Annunaki want to know as much information about each of us as possible. I will explain why later.

The Annunaki truly are Neters (watchers); they watch our every move, they track us, and they control us as needed. A testimony to this fact is found on our currency: the "all-seeing eye" found above the pyramid on our one dollar bills. Below the pyramid, we find "novus ordo seclorum" (New World Order). The New World Order begins after Jesus returns, wins the battle at Armageddon, and sets up his one-thousand-year reign. I believe that that one-thousand-year reign is the New World Order. As you will see later in this book, things in our world drastically change during the one-thousand-year reign of Jesus. The Annunaki track our movements; almost every new vehicle made today has some system like OnStar that can be used to locate us if needed. They want to know where we go and what we do. There are cameras everywhere nowadays tracking those movements. In many places they even know if you run a red light. Every telephone call (cellular or otherwise) can be monitored. They acquire a tremendous amount of information about our habits, interests, and numerous other things from our computers and use of the Internet.

I have no idea how the Annunaki are able to control our minds. I am convinced that they have the ability to do so, however. Fortunately, they have told us what to do in order for them not to be able to control our minds. The Bible says in John 8:32,

> And ye shall know the truth, and the truth shall make you free.

When a person understands who the Annunaki are and what they are doing, I do not think that the Annunaki can control their mind anymore. Of course, if you should become a problem for them, they will kill you.

I believe that the people who are the "Establishment" are leading characters in this human drama. And what is so clever that it almost boggles the human mind is, the characters in this play are not even aware that they are human proxies doing the will of their creators, the Annunaki.

Abraham, of Bible fame, seems to be just such a person. The Bible states that Abraham was approached by "angels of the lord." The word translated as angels in the Bible is *malachim*. The correct translation from Hebrew to English for this word *malachim* is "emissaries." The "angels of the lord" were simply emissaries of the Annunaki. The emissaries in the Bible almost always were airmen. They usually arrived on the scene in their flying machines that had wings (probably similar to a helicopter). They used all kinds of devices to deceive mankind. It is not surprising that the minds of ancient man would perceive them as being angels of the lord.

I have wondered for years why God would tell one of his children that he was his favorite, or his chosen one, who would receive all his inheritance. If I were wealthy and if I had several children and if I told one of them that he was my favorite (chosen one) and would receive

all my inheritance, what would that do? It would cause
the one chosen to feel that he was somehow better than
the others. It would cause the others to be jealous of
the one chosen and to be angry at me. It would ensure
that there would always be strife among my children. No
caring father would do that to his children.

Could it be that the Annunaki told that to Abraham in
order to guarantee that there would always be hostilities
between the children of Abraham? Christians, Jews, and
Muslims all consider Abraham to be "Father Abraham"
and their patriarch. Ishmael was Abraham's firstborn son,
just as Enki was Anu's firstborn son. Isaac was Abraham's
second son; Isaac's mother was Sarah who was also a half
sister of her husband, Abraham. Enlil was Anu's second
son; Enlil's mother was Antu who was also a half sister of
her husband, Anu. The feud between the half brothers
who were Annunaki (and their descendents) resulted
in one side using nuclear weapons against the other.
The spaceport that the Annunaki had built in the Sinai
Peninsula was nuked near the end of the twenty-first
century BCE. The mother of Abraham's firstborn son
was Hagar. The Bible says in Genesis 16:11–12,

> And the angel of the Lord said unto her, Behold,
> thou art with child, and shalt bear a son, and
> shalt call his name Ishmael; because the Lord
> hath heard thy affliction. And he will be a wild

man; his hand will be against every man, and
every man's hand against him; and he shall dwell
in the presence of all his brethren.

The feud between the descendents of Ishmael and Isaac
has now lasted about four thousand years. Will it culminate
in nuclear weapons being used again near the end of the
twenty-first-century AD? Abraham was simply the human
proxy who was "chosen" to play a role in the family feud
between the Annunaki half brothers. I am also quite sure
that Abraham is genetically linked to the Annunaki. If so,
the genetic link goes all the way back to the sons of the
gods cohabiting with the daughters of the Adam.

It is also nonsensical to believe that God would have any
reason to test Abraham. An all-knowing God would have
absolutely no reason to see whether Abraham was willing
to sacrifice his son Isaac. A true god would foreknow
the answer. However, the Annunaki had a great need to
know whether Abraham would carry out the instructions
they were to give him. If Abraham could be trusted, the
Annunaki were going to use him in great ways to further
their agenda; however, he needed to be tested first to
ensure that he would remain loyal.

The goal of the Annunaki to accumulate all the gold
on Earth is tremendously strengthened if they can keep
mankind constantly at odds with each other. If mankind
is constantly engaged in wars, petty quarrels, and so forth

instead of being focused on the more important affairs of daily living, it makes it much easier for the Annunaki to amass the gold and achieve their objective. Mankind should turn its focus on the Annunaki rather than on each other. Wars are also extremely profitable for the people and/or companies who own all the ammunition factories and associated companies who manufacture all the materials needed for wars. Do the Annunaki or their descendents own or control all these companies? I strongly suspect that they do.

Does the general populace benefit from wars? They do not. They are the ones who get killed fighting them. Leaders and heads of state may benefit from wars. If the war is won, they become national heroes, they become more powerful, and they become wealthy. Who are the leaders and heads of state? A very revealing verse is found concerning the leaders and heads of state in Daniel 4:17:

> This matter is by the decree of the watchers, and the demand by the word of the holy ones: to the intent that the living may know that the most High ruleth in the kingdom of men, and giveth it to whomsoever he will, and setteth up over it the basest of men.

The term used in the ancient texts to denote the sons of the gods who were involved in the shenanigans with the daughters of men is *watchers* (neter). *Neter* (watchers) is also the exact same word by which the Egyptians called their gods; the Egyptian gods were indeed the sons of Enki and Enlil and their descendents. It is clear that this verse says that the Annunaki give leadership of the kingdoms of men to whomsoever they choose. Who would decree that these rulers of the kingdoms of men be the basest of men? I certainly do not believe that God would. Are the Nefilim still present today? If so, I believe that they live underground; they may have the capability to watch us from there. But they obviously watch us from the skies as well. It would be next to impossible for their descendents not to be present on Earth today. Is mankind still being ruled by them today? I believe that we are. Are the rulers in our world today given their positions by the Annunaki? I believe that they are. And are the rulers of the kingdoms of men the basest of men? I believe that they are.

Why is our government so secretive about so many things? As a young man, I heard of something we refer to as the Roswell incident. The response of our government to this incident has always puzzled me. If an UFO actually crashed there, and if dead alien beings were found, why not tell the American people and indeed the whole world? Such an event would be a story of universal appeal and of extraordinary importance. The media could make tons of money covering such a story. Mankind would know for certain that other life-forms exist on places other than

Earth. Great knowledge would be gained by mankind by studying the spaceship and alien beings. If scientists and researchers from different disciplines of science were allowed to participate in such studies, marvelous advancements in knowledge and technology would surely occur. Why would anyone choose to keep such a secret? The only answer to that question that makes sense to me is someone whose own agenda might be exposed and/or someone who had a vested interest in keeping mankind dumbed down, i.e., the Annunaki.

Speaking of dumbed down, what about the Tower of Babel?

Genesis 11:3–4 says,

> And they said to one another, Go to let us make brick, and burn them thoroughly. And they had brick for stone, and slime had they for mortar. And they said, Go to, let us build us a city and a tower, whose top may reach unto heaven: and let us make us a name, lest we be scattered abroad upon the face of the whole earth.

The plain in Shinar where the humans had settled and where they tried to build their city and tower was the plain around Sumer. Sumer was the thriving metropolis of the day. The humans had been watching the Annunaki flying around in their flying machines. They had seen the Annunaki blast off in their spaceships from a "tower" whose top seemed to reach unto heaven because that is where the rocket ship went. They knew that they could be, as slaves, dispersed to any location on Earth if they did not gain favor with the Annunaki. The humans wanted to build a city, a launch tower, and a rocket ship to impress the Annunaki and gain their favor. The word for *name* in Hebrew is *shem*—*shem* can also mean *flying machine* or *rocket ship*, which is a more accurate translation here—"so that we may make a name for ourselves" should be translated into "so that we may make a rocket ship for ourselves."

The Annunaki did not want the humans to even try to build a city, a launch tower, or a rocket ship; the Annunaki obviously knew that the humans could not build a rocket ship. They also knew that such efforts would take them away from their work duties; and even in failure, they would gain knowledge. Why in the world would God, who knows everything, be in the least bit concerned about a newly created race of beings gaining a little knowledge? That is absurd.

The Annunaki did not take kindly to the efforts of the humans. A meeting was held. The suggestion was made to just kill all the humans who had been involved in the effort. However, one of the more powerful of the Annunaki thought that the humans could still be useful. He suggested that the humans simply be cut in half; that way, they would spend the rest of their lives with one-half trying to find its other half. The rest of the group thought that this was an ingenious plan. It was done. If we look at the human brain today, it appears as though the cerebral cortex has been cut in half. The neurosurgery, or whatever was done, did result in confusing the language and dumbing down the humans. This was also a way to create hostility between humans. We are simply not as friendly with people who we cannot talk to. It is interesting, to me, that our spiritual literature abounds with the idea of being made "whole" as we mature spiritually. I would love to see an Annunaki brain.

Back to Roswell, one could argue that no UFO or alien was found. If not, what harm could possibly come from a thorough investigation of what did happen? Would that not have been better than to have the public begin to distrust the government? Is the entire Roswell incident just another case of the Annunaki wanting to keep us dumbed down for as long as possible?

Is it advantageous for the government to have the citizens of the United States in disagreement about so many things? If we lived in peace and harmony, wouldn't we be a much more powerful nation? Couldn't we accomplish much more than we have? Why, then, wouldn't our government do everything possible to be truthful and answer our questions? Mark 3:25 says,

> And if a house be divided against itself, that house cannot stand.

What is the truth about the Roswell incident? What is the truth about the Kennedy assassination or that of his brother? What is the truth about the Illuminati, the Freemasons, or any other secret organization? What is the truth about 9/11? Did or did not a plane hit the Pentagon on that fateful day? Did or did not the Twin Towers collapse from a controlled demolition? It seems to me that any right-thinking person would agree that it would be beneficial to the government, our nation, and our citizens to be in agreement about the truth of these matters. Keeping us divided over issues is certainly of no benefit to our nation or to our people. It is, however, of tremendous benefit to any group that wants to maintain control over us so that we will continue to be good slaves and continue to be at odds with each other.

Was a master plan devised for us long ago and still being played out in our world today? Our own capital, Washington DC, was carefully designed and laid out by a secret organization, the Freemasons. Our first president, George Washington, was a member of that organization. Many of our subsequent presidents have been Freemasons. Why? Fifty-six men signed our Declaration of Independence. Fifty of them were Freemasons. As late as 1924, 60 percent of our senators were Masons. I am not suggesting that there is anything wrong with being a Mason; I was once a member myself. I am asking, why all the secrecy at the top levels of this organization and other so-called secret organizations? Isn't this secrecy harmful for all mankind because it breeds discord?

A very disturbing fact is that once a Mason reaches a certain level in the hierarchy, he takes an oath:

> I will aid and assist a companion Royal Arch Mason when engaged in any difficulty, and espouse his cause—whether it be right or wrong—a companion Royal Arch Mason's secrets shall remain as secure and inviolable, in my breast as in his own, murder and treason not excepted.

Murder and treason not excepted? Does it comfort your soul to know that so many of our presidents and senators have taken that oath? I can only hope that they were no better at keeping that oath than they have been at keeping the oath to uphold the Constitution.

Giuseppe Mazzini, once head of the Illuminati, said,

> We form an association of brothers in all points of the globe—Yet there is one unseen that can hardly be felt, yet it weighs on us. Whence comes it? Where is it? No one knows—or at least no one tells. This association is secret even to us the veterans of the Secret Societies.

That is an amazing statement when one realizes it came from the leader of one of the oldest, most powerful, and most secretive of organizations. Who is the one unseen? Could the Annunaki be the unseen power, and could they be unseen because they are controlling the Secret Societies from underground?

Another comment made in a letter that was not intended to get into public hands was made by Albert Pike. Mr. Pike was the person responsible for bringing the Scottish Rite portion of Freemasonry to the United States. He said,

> That which we say to the crowd is "we worship God"—The religion should be, by all us initiates of the high degrees, maintained in the purity of the Lucifer doctrine—Yes! Lucifer is God.

Lucifer actually means bearer or carrier of light. From the ancient texts we believe that Lucifer refers to Enki. Lucifer, Satan, and the devil are one and the same in the Bible. The Freemasons appear to believe in the Lucifer doctrine according to Mr. Pike. Enki was the one who founded what was probably the first secret society on planet Earth. It was called the Brotherhood of the Serpent. William Bramley, in his book *The Gods of Eden*, has done an excellent job of tracing the secret societies, beginning with the Brotherhood of the Serpent to the present.

The Brotherhood of the Serpent was a very influential group in ancient times. I believe that Enki formed this group in order to try to help his creation, mankind. The Brotherhood was dedicated to the dissemination and the attainment of spiritual knowledge. Enki knew that Enlil was unhappy about the fact that mankind had survived the flood; he also knew that Enlil was engaged in efforts that would deceive mankind. He knew that Enlil would cause the spiritual decay of mankind through dissemination of false information. The Brotherhood of the Serpent opposed the enslavement of spiritual beings. Even though Enki had created us to be slaves, he apparently did not believe that our spirituality should be destroyed. Enki had no problem with mankind working for the Annunaki; he knew that mankind should not be deluded into worshiping the Annunaki.

Enlil was able to defeat the efforts of Enki in this regard. The edited/altered version of this victory by Enlil is found in Genesis 3:13–15:

> And the Lord God said unto the woman, What is this that thou hast done? And the woman said, The serpent beguiled me, and I did eat. And the Lord God said unto the serpent, Because thou hast done this, thou art cursed above all cattle, and above every beast of the field; upon thou belly shalt thou go, and dust thou shalt eat all the

days of of thy life: And I will put enmity between thee and the woman, and between thy seed and her seed; it shall bruise thy head, and thou shalt bruise his heel.

"Dust thou shalt eat all the days of thy life" means that Enki was banished to Earth and could never return to Nibiru. He was given the epithets of Lucifer, Satan, the Devil, Evil Incarnate, Prince of Liars, and many more. Mankind was deceived into believing that he was so evil and so horrible that no right-thinking person would have anything to do with him.

Enlil was able to take over the control of the Brotherhood of the Serpent. He greatly altered the original goals and intentions of the group. He turned it into a chilling weapon of spiritual repression. The other secret societies that have occurred throughout history arose from the Brotherhood of the Serpent. These secret societies have been Enlil's most effective tool for maintaining spiritual decay, enslavement, and limitation of knowledge for mankind.

Why have we allowed all our money to be controlled by a "Federal Reserve Bank"? This is no federal bank. It operates totally independent from any governmental authority. It is not overseen or regulated by any branch of our government. It has to answer to no one (except the Annunaki). It is so secretive that we do not even know who all the people are who control it. How insane is that? A good slave should not ask such questions. A Republican senator from Pennsylvania, Louis McFadden, once said,

> We have in this country one of the most corrupt institutions the world has ever known. I refer to the Federal Reserve Board. This evil institution has impoverished the people of the United States—and has practically bankrupted our government. It has done this through the corrupt practices of the moneyed vultures who control it.

Thomas Jefferson put it another way:

> If the American people ever allow private banks to control the issue of their currency, first by inflation, then by deflation, the banks and the corporations which grow around them will deprive the people of all property until their children wake up homeless on the continent their fathers conquered.

Are the moneyed vultures who control our banks the Annunaki, descendents of the Annunaki, or servants of the Annunaki who just do what they are told to do?

Another of our past presidents, Woodrow Wilson, in
The New Freedom, says,

> Some of the biggest men in the United States,
> in the field of commerce and manufacture, are
> afraid of somebody, are afraid of something.
> They know there is a power somewhere so
> organized, so subtle, so watchful, so interlocked,
> so complete, so pervasive that they had better
> not speak above their breath when they speak in
> condemnation of it.

What human power could possibly be so organized,
so subtle, so watchful, so interlocked, so complete or so
pervasive? We have an extremely hard time putting ten
people in a room and getting them to agree on anything.
We should realize by now that the powers that be are not
the people we elect to office.

Julius Caesar said,

> Beware the leader who bangs the drum of war in
> order to whip the citizenry into a patriotic fervor,
> for patriotism is indeed a double-edged sword. It
> both emboldens the blood, just as it narrows the
> mind. And when the drums of war have reached
> a fever pitch, and the blood boils with hate and
> the mind has closed, the leader will have no

need in seizing the rights of the citizenry. Rather, the citizenry, infused with fear and blinded by patriotism, will offer up all of their rights unto the leader, and gladly so. How do I know? This is what I have done. And I am Caesar.

That is exactly what George W. Bush did to the American people after 9/11. Deceit and lies were the order of the day. There were no weapons of mass destruction. Iraq was no threat to the United States, but his tactic worked. During the furor and confusion, Bush gave a bill to the congressmen and senators one hour before they had to go and vote on it. He told them that they must pass it for national security reasons. The bill was 342 pages long and is called "the Patriot Act." Not a single member of our legislature had time to read it, much less study it. But they passed it. It is, perhaps, the most hideous piece of legislation ever enacted by our legislature, and they have passed a lot of bad ones. Bush then convinced the American people to go to war (even though it was done illegally without the consent of congress). Among other horrors, one of the things that the Patriot Act says is that the government is free to "disappear" you if any terrorist intent might be inferred from your conduct. This means that if the government infers from your conduct whatever they want to infer, they do not have to notify your family, your lawyer, or anybody else; they can just "disappear" you. No due process is required. Talk about gladly handing over your rights to the leader.

Following his presidency, Bush was asked whether some of these decisions were in the best interest of the American people. He refused to answer but smugly stated that he was happy to have served. I do not know whether George W. Bush realizes that legislation like this is very harmful to mankind but very helpful to the Annunaki agenda. He is a member of the secret society Skull and Bones. We have recently found out that the number-one priority of this very old and very secretive organization is to form a coalition that will one day rule the world.

Arthur S. Miller, a law professor at George Washington University, wrote about our government:

> Those who formally rule take their signals and commands not from the electorate as a body, but from a small group of men (plus a few women). This group will be called the Establishment. It exists even though that existence is strongly denied. It is one of the secrets of the American social order. A second secret is the fact that the existence of the Establishment—the ruling class—is not supposed to be discussed.

Are the Establishment descendents of the Annunaki or people doing their bidding? We do know that the

George Bush family is certainly part of the Establishment; we also know that the Bush family has worked hard for One World Order for several generations. We know that the Bush family is blood related to at least twenty of the kings and queens of Europe. We also know who put these people on their thrones. It is pretty easy to understand why the Establishment does not want the slaves to discuss this matter. I have seen estimates that there are about one hundred families, and their descendents, who now own about 75 percent of the wealth of the entire world. I doubt that the members of these families realize who they really are or understand why they have been so fortunate. I strongly suspect that the reason for their good fortune is genetic. They are probably descendents of the children who were originally one-half Annunaki and one-half human.

Another of our presidents, Gerald Ford (who also served as senator and vice president), in a written statement, said,

> I have tried as senator, vice president, and as president to have the matter of UFOs thoroughly investigated, but it was never approved by the official authorities.

Are you telling me, President Ford, that the president of the United States of America cannot get an investigation done if some higher authorities do not want it done? Who are these higher authorities?

Ronald Reagan claimed to have spotted UFOs on two different occasions during his life. Perhaps that spurred his interest in Star Wars defense. At any rate, I believe that President Reagan understood economics. I believe that he also tried to limit the Federal Reserve Board's power, but I also believe that he became frustrated when he could accomplish so little in this regard. He did make a statement to the General Assembly of the United Nations:

> Our differences would disappear if we were invaded by an alien presence, but isn't it obvious that an alien presence is already amongst us?

I do not think that President Reagan knew who the alien presence is, but I do believe that he recognized the influence of the Annunaki on the White House.

Our mainstream media is both a joke and a nightmare. Practically everything that we see, hear, or read has to be taken with a huge grain of salt. There is little honesty or truth in what we are being exposed to day after day. We sit in front of our TV, read our newspapers and magazines, listen to our radios, and continue to get dumbed down more and more day after day. That is the nightmare. The joke is on us. We do not even realize, in most cases, what is happening to us. It is impossible for us to make good decisions with inaccurate information. Alas, the Annunaki are so much more intelligent than we are. The corporations who control the media impose fairly strict censorship upon what can be released to the public. Who controls all these sources of our information? Who are the owners and CEOs of these corporations? The Establishment elite own the corporations, run our government, run our banking system, and run the world. Are they descendents of the Annunaki or influenced, in some way, to do their bidding?

We should also realize that the master planners have used religion as one of their strongest tools with which to manipulate us. What better way to keep mankind at odds with each other could there be than the ways in which our religions have accomplished it? Every religion in existence today promotes beliefs that cause discord between humans. The Koran even encourages murder of the infidels if they do not agree to convert to Islam.

James 1:26–27 says,

> If any man among you seem to be religious, and brideleth not his tongue, but deceiveth his own heart, this man's religion is vain. Pure religion and undefiled before God and the Father is this, To visit the fatherless and widows in their affliction, and to keep himself unspotted from the world.

We do deceive our own hearts by trusting the false doctrines taught by all religions. We are quick to become hypocritical about the beliefs of others.

The televangelists are really a sad joke on humanity. In 2 Timothy 4:3–4 we find the following:

> For the time will come when they will not endure sound doctrine; but after their own lusts shall they heap to themselves teachers, having itching ears; And they shall turn away their ears from the truth, and shall be turned into fables.

What are teachers who have itching ears? They are teachers who teach what their flock wants to hear. They have no regard for sound doctrine or the truth. In order to stay on television, one must raise a lot of money. In order to raise a lot of money, one must teach what the flock wants to hear. The flock wants to hear that they are one of the ones chosen by God to spend eternity with him. The flock wants to hear that they will be safe and secure for all eternity because they believe some particular doctrine. The flocks will not send in their money unless they are taught the beliefs that have been ingrained into them since childhood (such as they are God's chosen people). Sound doctrine is not what they have been taught as children nor is it what they want to hear. Folks, if you want to listen to them and watch them, go ahead. But please quit sending them money, and do not buy their books, CDs, DVDs, or anything else they are selling. That will only help the Annunaki to continue the deception and maintain control of mankind. How many wars have been fought on this Earth over religion? I do not know, but it is a ridiculously large number (especially when one is too many). The Nefilim are very wise, but like us, they are not always merciful.

We have numerous pictures of UFOs that are coming out of an ocean or water of some kind. The fact that UFOs exist seems indisputable today. We have had so many sightings of UFOs; how could all of them be coming from outer space? Is it possible that many of the UFO sightings (perhaps all of them) are actually the Annunaki coming up from their underground facilities to check on their project, to alter something, or for whatever need they might have?

The idea that an alien race came to planet Earth long ago and that they still dominate us today is certainly not original with me. Perhaps the first writer of the twentieth century to write about this was Charles Hoy Fort (1867–1923). William Bramley (1989) in his book entitled *The Gods of Eden* reached the same conclusion that Fort did:

> Human beings appear to be a slave race languishing on an isolated planet in a small galaxy. As such, the human race was once a

source of labor for an extraterrestrial civilization and still remains a possession today. To keep control over its possession, that civilization has bred never-ending conflict between human beings, has promoted spiritual decay and has erected on Earth conditions of unremitting physical hardship. This situation has existed for thousands of years and it continues today.

Are these authors correct? They certainly are. There are so many things occurring today that make no sense; however, when these things are viewed with an understanding of the Annunaki agenda, they make perfectly good sense.

I could go through the Bible and point out story after story that is very deceptive. Each of these stories serves the agenda of the Annunaki, and the explanations given to mankind about what these verses mean are extremely difficult to believe. I will take the time, at this point in my book, to discuss only one of these stories. I believe that the following discussion will make my point. Each person who reads this book can then make their own decisions about what is fact and what is purely deception about the Bible. The story that I want to discuss is known as the Exodus.

I was taught as a child, and mankind is supposed to believe, that God chose a group of people as his favorites, allowed them to become slaves in Egypt, rescued them from the hands of the pharaoh, made them wander around in a desert for forty years, and then refused to give them the reward (I shall call the reward a "lollipop" since the whole concept is so childish) that he had promised them. I have discussed, in an earlier chapter, the reasons why I think it very unlikely that any loving father would tell one of his children that he/she was his favorite. I certainly do not believe that God would do such a thing. God would have no reason to put the Israelites through the shenanigans that they were put through. However, Enlil had chosen the Israelites to be his human proxies. Enlil needed to convince the Israelites that he was the Supreme Being. Enlil also needed to test the Israelites, just as he had Abraham, to ensure that they had fallen for the deception. He wanted to be sure that the Israelites would follow his instructions. The Israelites were simply hard to convince.

Children learn many of their behavior patterns from their parents. Later in our lives, some of our behavior is based on what we have seen others do. The Israelites had observed the behavior of the Annunaki for several generations. I am sure that some very interesting stories had been passed around. When the Israelites sinned, had their orgies, or disobeyed Yahweh in some way, I strongly suspect that there were times that they were just mimicking behaviors they had seen from the Annunaki.

I do not believe that this generation of Israelites ever believed that they were dealing with the Supreme Being. No one would defy Yahweh as many times as the Israelites did if they thought that there was any possibility that they were dealing with the Supreme Being. Finally we are supposed to believe that Yahweh told his children that he alone would decide whether they were going to spend eternity in paradise with him or in the lake of fire separated from him, but because they had sinned (just like all mankind had sinned), he was not going to give them the "lollipop" he had promised them. The Israelites were not allowed to enter the promised land. It is absolutely ridiculous to believe that God would behave in such a childish manner.

The Bible says that this group was not allowed to enter the promised land because they had been disobedient to Yahweh's word. The real reason that they were not allowed in was that the Annunaki had not been able to convince them of the supremacy of Enlil, and the Annunaki knew that they could not trust the Israelites to carry out their instructions. The instructions were anything but godly, i.e., they were instructed to go into the land and kill every man, woman, and child.

The Annunaki were simply trying to ensure that the Israelites could be trusted to continue the family feud that they were so masterfully manipulating. Enlil and his descendents had simply recruited Abraham and his descendents through the line of Isaac and Jacob to continue the family feud against Enki and his descendents who possessed the Land of Canaan. The family feud can be traced, if one is so inclined, right through the Old Testament to the birth of Jesus. The feud then continues to be outlined in the New Testament. The Revelation to St. John describes the culmination of this horrific feud that has lasted for so many thousands of years.

Chapter 5

WHAT IS UNDERGROUND?

I have stated that it is possible that the Annunaki have built underground accommodations for themselves. Actually I think that it is quite likely that they have. If such accommodations do exist, I doubt they are what most readers of this book might envision them to be. I believe that their underground civilization would more closely resemble the Garden of Eden than it would some dark, damp cave. I strongly suspect that it would be magnificent and quite an underground paradise. In the January 2011 edition of the *National Geographic* magazine, there is an article and pictures of an enormous cave found in Vietnam. This cave has an underground river, jungle, and even clouds. It is quite amazing.

The ancient texts mention a granddaughter of Enlil, named Ereshkigal, who became the mistress of the lower world. After the lots were cast and Enki had become Lord Waters, he took Ereshkigal to the lower world. A son of Enki had offended Ereshkigal by being impolite to one of her counselors. This son of Enki was named Nergal. He was sent to the lower world to apologize to Ereshkigal. The ancient texts describe Ereshkigal's domain as being far away and difficult to reach, a "restricted area" but not a "place of no return." Upon Nergal's arrival, he was escorted to Ereshkigal's "wide courtyard." He later saw her taking her daily bath, one thing led to another, and Nergal spent the next seven days and nights making love to Ereshkigal. There is no mention in any of the ancient texts that this was a hellish experience for either party involved. After quite a soap opera, Nergal married Ereshkigal and became lord of the lower world. Their home was later described as being

> a bright and fruitful home in the subterranean paradise called "mouth of the rivers," which was closely associated with the home of Enki in the Apsu.

This text definitely states that Ereshkigal and Nergal, the mistress and lord of the lower world, had a magnificent home that is located underground.

There is also a description in one of the ancient texts of Enki taking a journey to the Apsu. During the journey, he has this to say,

> To thee, Apsu, pure land,
> Where great waters rapidly flow,
> To the Abode of Flowing Waters
> Enki in the pure waters established;
> In the midst of the Apsu,
> A great sanctuary he established.

To my way of thinking, the pure waters are underground; the "Abode of Flowing Waters" could be the southern tip of Africa, I suppose. But I believe that the Apsu is underground, and that it is a great sanctuary.

I believe that the Apsu also contains the abyss, bottomless pit, and hell that are spoken of in the Bible. Perhaps, this part of the underground civilization is more like what most of us envision it to be. A passage in one of the ancient texts that is about five thousand years old describes a person named Enkidu. He was given a death sentence; he would have to spend the rest of his life on "death row." A person with a human body and a birdlike face was going to take Enkidu to the place where he would spend the rest of his life. Enkidu was told,

He will be dressed like an Eagle; by the arm he will lead thee. "Follow me," he will say; he will lead you to the House of Darkness, The abode below the ground; the abode which none leave who have entered into it. A road from which there is no return; a house whose dwellers are bereft of light, where dust is in their mouths and clay is their food.

It would seem that this underground civilization encompasses all facets of life and death that are found on the surface.

I mentioned earlier that we had found huge excavations with what appeared to be apartment buildings eight stories tall that could accommodate fifty thousand inhabitants. There were also niches in the caverns containing huge sarcophagi that weighed over sixty tons. Allow me to speculate some more. What were the apartments and sarcophagi for? A god (Annunaki) would not live in such a place. I suspect that the apartments were for human slaves. They needed slaves to do the underground work, also. Unfortunately, I also strongly suspect that the sarcophagi were for humans. I would not be surprised if, by now, there have not been many generations of human slaves who have been born and bred underground and have never seen the surface of this planet. I am quite curious to know, if this premise is correct, what their average life span is. Their life spans may have become quite long compared to ours since they are not exposed to sunlight. If so, and in light of what is in store for us who are on the surface, the underground might be the next hot spot to move to. After all, if one is a slave, what difference does it make whether you are slaving above or below ground?

In book two of the Earth Chronicles entitled *The Stairway to Heaven,* there are descriptions of journeys that began aboveground, moved under the ground where amazing descriptions of places as well as beings are found, and culminated with being put in a rocket ship and sent to some heavenly abode. I believe that the underground civilization does exist; I believe that it is inhabited today. There is no reason to believe that it does not include every aspect of civilization that we have on the surface. Parts of it must be very similar to the Garden of Eden, parts of it must be inhabited by common slaves (like me), and parts of it must be quite hellish.

We know that Washington DC was planned and laid out by the Freemasons. I wonder what is under Washington DC. This underground stuff, of course, is pure speculation. But something seems to be coming from somewhere that greatly influences what is happening aboveground. In *The Gods of Eden,* a book written by William Bramley, in chapter 35 entitled "St. Germain Returns" there is a description of an underground disc, which is supposed to be used for mind control of surface inhabitants on Earth:

> A disc of gold at least twelve feet in diameter. Filling it so that the points touched the circumference blazed a seven point star composed entirely of yellow diamonds, a solid mass of brilliant golden Light.

Guy Warren Ballard, a mining engineer, claimed to have seen this machine in the 1930s. He says that the machine was deep within a mountain in Northern California. He was told that the forces emitted by the machine were directed "to the humanity of Earth" and that

> this radiation affects the seven ganglionic centers within every human body on our planet as well as all animal and plant life.

The only other thing that I have to say about this is that the minds in Washington DC that are involved in our political process are not functioning correctly.

I believe that Enki is living underground today in the AB.ZU. I do not know whether he is running the world and controlling mankind from his facilities there or whether Enlil is in control from Nibiru. I do know that right-thinking humans are not in control.

Chapter 6

GENETIC ENGINEERING

Genetics is the study of genes. Deoxyribonucleic acid (DNA) is a nucleic acid that contains the genetic instructions for the development and functioning of all living organisms. Within cells, DNA is organized into long structures called chromosomes. Chromosomes are duplicated before cells divide. The set of chromosomes in a cell make up its genome. Genes are segments of DNA that carry specific genetic information that is transcribed. Genetic information is held within genes; a gene is a unit of heredity that influences a particular characteristic in an organism. The human genome has approximately three billion base pairs arranged into forty-six chromosomes.

DNA can be damaged or altered by many substances such as oxidizing agents, alkylating agents, and high-energy electromagnetic radiation such as x-rays and ultraviolet light. To alter three billion base pairs and to test the result of each alteration would be a tremendous undertaking.

The Annunaki created man in their own image and likeness to be slaves. I quote from the creation epic the words of Marduk, a son of Enki:

> I will produce a lowly Primitive; "Man" shall be his name.
> I will create a Primitive Worker; He will be charged with the service of the gods, that they might have their ease.

Ancient man, the man of the Bible, did not worship his god; he worked for him. The word in the Bible that has been translated as worship is *avod* (work). When mankind began to multiply so rapidly after receiving the ability to procreate, the Annunaki realized that they needed a better way to control them. As Enlil had stated, mankind was too noisy and boisterous.

The Annunaki called themselves gods; however, they believed that there was a Supreme Being who had created them. They decided that they would have the slaves worship them as God, rather than only work for them. That was very clever. The Annunaki would have the best of both worlds, so to speak; mankind would worship them as gods and continue to work for them as slaves. By having mankind worship them, they could pound into our little brains that we must obey them. The concept eventually evolved into having mankind believe that the Annunaki were Yahweh, God, Allah—a monotheistic deity. By creating this deception, they were able to manipulate, coerce, and control the noisy, boisterous critters better. There is scripture that tells us when the Annunaki devised this scheme. It is found in Genesis 4:25–26:

> And Adam knew his wife again; and she bare a son, and called his name Seth: For God, said she, hath appointed me another seed instead of Abel, whom Cain slew. And to Seth, to him also was born a son; and he called his name Enos: then began men to call upon the name of the Lord.

When mankind began to call upon the name of the Lord is when Enlil's scheme began to be successful. Mankind began to worship the Annunaki during the time of Enos (Enosh in many translations). Enosh was born 98,260 years ago.

The ancient texts vividly describe how the Adam was created. The egg or DNA from ape-woman was mixed with clay, bitumens, and the essence of the blood (not the sperm) from a young Annunaki male. The mixture was placed in a series of purifying baths. This apparently caused the DNA from ape-woman to combine with the

DNA from the Annunaki male. In some way the genes from the male were imprinted upon this embryo. The embryo that was produced was implanted into the womb of Ninki (Enki's wife). The ancient texts say that ten months later the baby was delivered by cesarean section. The "mold" that was used to create the Adam was then used to create seven more males and seven females. The females were made out of the essence or mold of Adam. Ninki became known as Ninti. Ti means rib. Ninti was the lady of the rib. The biblical description of the event is found in Genesis 2:21–22:

> And the Lord God caused a deep sleep to fall upon Adam, and he slept: and he took one of his ribs, and closed up the flesh instead thereof; And the rib, which the Lord God had taken from man, made he a woman, and brought her unto the man.

Eve or females were made out of the mold or essence of Adam, but the edited/altered versions that are in the Bible are very deceptive and misleading. We also find in the Bible in Genesis 2:7:

> And the Lord God formed man of the dust of the ground, and breathed into his nostrils the breath of life; and man became a living soul.

Clay was used to create Adam, not dust; the inerrant word of God also fails to mention the other ingredients that were used, i.e., DNA from the egg of ape-woman, blood from an Annunaki male and bitumens (we don't know exactly what that was). In one of the ancient texts, Enki gave the following instructions to the Mother Goddess (his half sister, Ninharsag):

> Mix to the core a clay from the basement of Earth,
> just above the Abzu—and shape it into the form of
> a core. I shall provide good, knowing young gods
> who will bring that clay to the right condition.

This was not just any old clay; it certainly was not dust. In Hebrew, the term *adama* means dark-red soil or earth; also, the word *nephesh* means spirit or soul. In the Hebrew Bible, mankind is repeatedly told by Yahweh not to eat or drink blood because it is the nephesh. Blood was also an essential ingredient for the creation of Adam. We find from one of the ancient texts:

> In the clay, god and Man shall be bound, to a unity
> brought together; So that to the end of days the Flesh
> and the Soul which in a god have ripened—that
> Soul in a blood-kinship be bound; as its Sign life
> shall proclaim. So that this not be forgotten, let the
> Soul in a blood-kinship be bound.

I believe that this text is saying that Annunaki blood was mixed into the clay so as to bind the Annunaki and man genetically and that both the flesh (image) and the soul (likeness) of the Annunaki would become imprinted upon man in a kinship that would not be broken until the end of days. The blood-kinship that would last to the end of days may be the kinship linking Enlil to his part-human son, Jesus. Please note, however, that the ancient text implies that the blood-kinship will be broken at the end of days.

The biological process by which living organisms reproduce is very complex to us humans. We have made some progress. We began by taking sperm from a male, placing it into the vagina of a female at the appropriate time during the menstrual cycle, and thus caused pregnancy; this process is called artificial insemination.

Next we learned how to take an egg from a female, place it in a container with sperm from a male, and have fertilization occur. The fertilized egg developed into an embryo. We call this process in vitro fertilization (fertilization outside of the body). The embryo is implanted into the womb of a female, maturation occurs, and the baby is delivered. We sometimes call these children test tube babies. There are many such individuals in our world today; I think that some of them are in their thirties now.

During the past decade or so, we have been able to clone animals. The principle is the same as taking a cutting from a plant and reproducing a duplicate of that same plant. The process was first demonstrated by removing the nucleus of a fertilized egg from a frog and replacing it with another nucleus (unfertilized) from the same frog. The egg developed and produced another identical frog. The same principle could be applied to human beings; the result would be an exact duplicate of that human being.

We have now developed a process that we call cell fusion. In this process, cells from two different sources are fused together (the two sources could be a human and some other animal) to form one "supercell." When the supercell splits, the mixture of nuclei and chromosomes may split in a completely different pattern than either of the original two cells. The result would be neither a human nor the other animal. The new creature would have characteristics and traits of both. I believe that this is exactly what the Annunaki did after creating the Adam (sterile). The birth goddess process was too slow. Genetic engineering experiments were performed in order to produce a suitable slave who might then be cloned. This would produce numerous slaves very rapidly.

There was a Babylonian priest/historian in the third century BCE who wrote that the god Belus brought forth beings that were produced by a twofold principle:

Men appeared with two wings, some with four and two faces. They had one body but two heads, the one of a man, the other of a woman. They were likewise in their several organs both male and female. Other human figures were to be seen with the legs and horns of goats. Some had horses' feet; others had the limbs of a horse behind, but in front were fashioned like men, resembling hippocentaurs. Bulls likewise bred there with the heads of men; and dogs with fourfold bodies, and the tails of fishes. Also horses with the heads of dogs; men too and other animals with the heads and bodies of horses and the tails of fishes. In short, there were creatures with the limbs of every species of animals—Of all these were preserved in the temple of Belus at Babylon.

In the Egyptian hieroglyphics, we see men with heads of birds as well as many other mixtures of men and animals. There are millions of statues of all kinds of hideous creatures such as gargoyles found on all kinds of buildings and other places all over our world today. Perhaps the Sphinx is a testimony to this attempt at genetic engineering.

There are many stories about a female creature that may have been the result of some such genetic experiment;

her name was Lilith. She had wings and birdlike feet. Her name meant "she of the night" and "the howler." Her expertise was enticing men to their death and snatching newborns from their mother. In Jewish legends, she was said to hate men because she was supposed to have been the intended bride of Adam, but she was rejected in favor of Eve. In older Sumerian tales, she was the consort of an evil birdlike creature named Anzu, was called "the dark maid," and was said to have "fled to wild, uninhabited places." At any rate, I have no doubt that the Annunaki tried many different mixtures in order to try to come up with the perfect slave. In a way, I guess that mankind was fortunate that no better slave could be produced. It is possible that some of these creatures are being held in the bottomless pit or abyss to be unleashed upon mankind during the Great Tribulation.

The Bible is a story about the Annunaki; it is also a story about a crazy family feud between two half brothers. But it is also much more than that. It is a fantastic story about genetic engineering, and that is the most important aspect of the entire book.

I have said earlier that Adam, the one who could procreate, was created about 112,360 years ago and that he lived for 54,180 years. The story of the creation of this Adam is true. However, this Adam, in terms of the genetic experiment that was being performed by the Annunaki, represents Neanderthal man. It was not the individual

who was initially created who lived 54,180 years; that
was the number of years that Neanderthal man roamed
Earth.

There were three branches of people who descended
from the Neanderthals. They were not natural descendents.
The Annunaki genetically altered some Neanderthals in
order to produce a branch of Cain, a branch of Abel, and
a branch of Seth. The people of the branch of Cain were
apparently quite fierce and savage. They killed off the branch
of Abel. There is a lot of evidence now that the people of
Cain were rounded up and transported to South America.
They became the Aztecs, Mayas, and Incas. These people
had genetic traits that caused them to be quite savage.
They indulged in human sacrifices, cannibalism, and the
like. The branch of Seth was then genetically altered by the
Annunaki to produce the branch of Enosh.

I have stated earlier that Enosh was born 98,260 years
ago and that he lived 54,300 years. Enosh, in terms of
the genetic experiment, represents Cro-Magnon man;
they survived for 54,300 years. If you recall, man began to
call on the name of the Lord and worship the Annunaki
during the time of Enosh. Cro-Magnon men were the
first to worship the Annunaki. Cro-Magnon man was not
very intelligent; they were easily deceived. I am not sure
what our excuse is.

Each of the names of the people described in the fifth
chapter of Genesis (until it gets to Noah) represents a

branch of people who had been altered genetically from the previous group (perhaps by as little as one gene). If you read the fifth chapter of Genesis, you will see that the age of Noah is not given like the others were. We are not told how old Noah was when he had his first son either. Noah was an actual person. The Annunaki were keeping very detailed records concerning these people, thus the long lists of genealogies that we find in the Bible.

Enki, the greatest scientist of the Annunaki, knew that Noah had received special genetics. He did not want to end the experiment and have to start over because of the flood.

The experiment continues today. That is why the Annunaki want to know as much as possible about you. That is also what many of the UFO abductions are all about. The Annunaki are tinkering with and fine-tuning their experiment. Their goal in this experiment, like it was when they produced the first sterile Adam, is to produce the perfect slave.

I said in the first chapter of this book that the grandest deception had far-reaching implications. I would like to describe a few of those at this time. Like all experiments, the result is not known. There are times that we are greatly surprised by the outcome of an experiment because it is so different from what we expected. Like many experiments, both good and bad outcomes can occur.

The genetic engineering experiment that the Annunaki are conducting has resulted in some humans receiving genes that give them exceptional talents. Such talents include outstanding mental, physical, and psychological capabilities. Interestingly, there is a reality TV show presently running that is titled *Superhumans.* Humans with amazing abilities are highlighted. Unfortunately, some people receive genes that have caused mental retardation, all kinds of birth defects, and all kinds of illnesses. Many of these things would have never occurred in the process of evolution. They have occurred because the Annunaki were experimenting. The vast majority of the people on this planet has received genes that have produced the negative aspects of humanity; in comparison, only a few have received the positive talents and capabilities. I believe that the ratio favoring the negative is far out of balance for what it should be for the process of natural selection. If the normal evolutionary process were being followed, mankind would have far more positive traits than we find in our world today.

The Annunaki have put many chemicals in our food, our water, and our atmosphere in order to test the outcomes. Our pharmaceutical industry has been greatly damaged because of the genetic experiment. Drugs are not designed and produced in most instances for the betterment of mankind. They are designed and produced, more often than not, in order to test some aspect of the huge experiment in genetic engineering that is taking place.

There is no question that the experiment has produced extreme physical hardships on mankind that were unnecessary; emotional distress of unbearable excess has also been unnecessary. But I believe that the most devastating aspect of the experiment is the numbing down of our conscious.

We have things like drive-by shootings where people are killed for no reason, many instances of atrocities occurring just for the thrill of it, and numerous examples of mankind's disregard for human life. Many of these things were unheard of (like drive-by shootings) just a few years ago. Serial killings where individuals go on rampages for no reason are becoming more frequent. In spite of our constant wars and disagreements, I think that there is one thing that almost all mankind would agree on, and that is that man is no better today at loving and caring for his fellow man than we were when the people of Cain killed the people of Abel.

It is quite ironic that the fate of mankind may have been determined by a "roll of the dice." When the lots were cast, if Enki (that old devil) had won and become "Lord of the Command," the fate of mankind would have been much different. Enki believed that we should be allowed to grow spiritually and not be deceived about spiritual matters. He even formed the Brotherhood of the Serpent in order to help mankind attain spiritual knowledge. Another real irony is that mankind has been led to believe that Enki (the devil) is out to destroy mankind and that Jesus is our savior; nothing could be further from the truth.

One's fate can be altered. Genetic research being performed today (by humans) seems to indicate that human cells have the potential to live for extremely long periods of time. They may live forever if given the proper nutrition ("Food of Life") and hydration ("Water of Life").

Perhaps the largest laboratory for the genetic engineering experiment that exists on the surface of Earth can be found in the state of Utah. It is called the Church of Jesus Christ of Latter-day Saints (the Mormons). To anyone who has studied the history of the Mormon Church or the book of Mormon, it should be quite obvious today that the visitations to Joseph Smith (Moroni et al.) were from the Annunaki. Through the Mormon Church, the Annunaki have set up an almost perfect laboratory for their experiment.

The genealogical records kept by the Mormons, and needed by the Annunaki for their experiment, are not kept aboveground, however. This is the largest genealogical library in the world, and the vaults are housed about twenty miles south of Salt Lake City. They are in one of the mountains in the Rocky Mountain Range. They are protected by mountain granite that is seven-hundred-feet thick and by a steel door that weighs fourteen tons. These vaults will survive the natural disaster that is to come.

The strong family ties and inbreeding, if I may call it that, of the Mormons is a good thing. The Annunaki attempted to have the ancient Israelites of biblical times do the same thing. That makes it easier to document and control their experiment. The spiritual teachings of the Mormons, however, are very harmful to mankind. The Mormons teach that "God" will eliminate the "spirit world" entirely. They teach that mankind will exist solely as a material being in a material universe.

Creating humans without a spirit or soul is exactly what the Annunaki are trying to achieve with their genetic experiment. If the Annunaki are successful in eliminating the spirit and soul of man, they will have created the perfect slave, a dumbed-down biological robot.

The Church of Jesus Christ of Latter-day Saints has accumulated great wealth. The members of that church have accomplished great things. Unfortunately, the Mormons have not realized that they have been deceived by the Annunaki. The Annunaki never intended for mankind to partake of the "Tree of Knowledge." Once that occurred, the Annunaki have done everything they could to limit the knowledge of mankind. Humans have achieved basically what the Annunaki need for us to achieve in order to further their agenda. The Mormons should rethink their position, just as all religions should, in light of the new knowledge we have about the Annunaki.

Zecharia Sitchin was the first to identify and write about the Annunaki in modern times. William Bramley advanced our knowledge about them and their activities. Others are beginning to understand more about the Annunaki. We have identified both our creator and our enemy.

Chapter 7

WHAT HAPPENS NEXT?

The Annunaki came here looking for gold. They may have already sent most of the gold ever formed on Earth back to Nibiru; however, a large amount of gold still remains on this planet. I believe that they have every intention of finishing the job. They have developed ingenious ways of obtaining the gold. Because of their long life spans, they can also be very patient. I want to explain just one of the ingenious ways in which they have obtained a large amount of gold right here in the United States. They allowed slaves to discover it, recover it from the earth, and use it for a short while. They set up our banking system and convinced us to give gold to the federal government with which to back our currency. They then convinced us that our currency needed no backing, and they confiscated all our gold.

They allowed us to pay for and build Fort Knox, a place where we could store the gold. They then loaned us so much paper that they said they needed some collateral on the loans they had made. As collateral for the loans (a large part of our national debt), we gladly put up all the gold in Fort Knox. The United States government no longer owns that gold; the Annunaki or their agents own it. As might be expected, however, you and I and the rest of the taxpayers pay for storing it, guarding it, and maintaining it until the Annunaki are ready to use it. One would think that it will be sent back to Nibiru (more on that later). By the way, they also allow us to pay all the expenses incurred in printing, storing, and distributing all the paper that they loan to us. I told you that they are much smarter than we are.

I bought my first gold coin, a one-ounce Krugerrand, over thirty years ago for $132. The price of gold has increased over the years. One ounce now costs more than $1,300. It is interesting to me, that during those thirty years, there has never been a large market for gold. It could always be bought and sold, but there was never a concerted effort by anyone to purchase a lot of it. Today, when the price of gold is at an all-time high, someone is trying to buy all they can. There is an advertisement every few minutes on TV that someone will buy your gold. Being the suspicious person that I am, I think that I know who will end up with all this gold. I also am quite sure that I know what the Annunaki will do with it. You will find out later in this book.

The American people will eventually wake up. When they realize how government and religion have been used to deceive them, they will be very confused. When they realize how the Federal Reserve banking system has been used to bankrupt them, they will be very angry. When they become angry enough, broke enough, and hungry enough, there will be civil unrest, rioting, and looting. There may even be attempts to overthrow the government and throw the scoundrels out. The Annunaki, their descendents, or their agents (whoever is running our world) have already made preparations for this.

It has been estimated that there are over two thousand *FEMA detention centers* already built and in operation in this country. These remind me of Nazi concentration camps of the past. The excuse for having these detention centers is, according to our government, to have a place to detain terrorists in case we are attacked. Come on, man. There is no way two thousand such places could ever be needed for terrorists. They will be used to incarcerate American citizens when we finally rebel. What is even more frightening is that over one million little plastic or fiber glass coffins have also been built and readied for the rebellion. The American taxpayer, of course, pays for both the detention centers and the coffins. The Annunaki have manipulated the circumstances so that the slave pays for the prison in which he is incarcerated, the weapons with which he is killed, and the coffin in which he is buried.

In one of Sitchin's books entitled *Genesis Revisited,* he revealed an incident called the Phobos incident. It concerned the loss of a Soviet spacecraft sent to explore Mars. A thought-to-be-hollow moonlet of Mars is called Phobos. Two Soviet probes had been launched in 1988 to reach Mars in 1989. The first probe just vanished. No explanation for the sudden disappearance was ever given. The second probe reached Mars and began sending back photographs while in Martian orbit. A cigar-shaped object was seen flying between the probe and surface of Mars. As the probe aligned itself with the moonlet, Phobos, its last picture was sent. The last picture was that of a missile headed toward the probe from the moonlet. The probe was destroyed. We know that the Annunaki had an outpost on Mars that was used as a relay station between Earth and Nibiru. It may be that that relay station has been moved underground into the hollow moonlet where it is still being used today.

It is common practice among the occult to tell the victim of their impending murder or sacrifice. There has been much speculation about what the Bible calls the Great Tribulation. The Annunaki may be telling us that they will torture mankind for three and a half years. After the torture, they will have a great war and kill a bunch of us at the foot of Mount Megiddo, Har-Megiddo, Armageddon. They apparently have some real treats in store for mankind during the Great Tribulation. Mankind will suffer some horrible atrocities. I am not going to take the time to write about all the atrocities. I will quote one that comes from Revelation 9:1–6:

> And the fifth angel sounded, and I saw a star fall from heaven unto the earth; and to him was given the key of the bottomless pit. And he opened the bottomless pit; and there arose a smoke out of the pit, as the smoke of a great furnace; and the sun and the air were darkened by reason of the smoke of the pit. And their came out of the smoke locusts upon the earth; and unto them was given power, as the scorpions of the earth have power. And it was commanded them that they should not hurt the grass of the earth, neither any green thing, neither any tree; but only those men which have not the seal of God on their foreheads. And to them it was given that they should not kill them, but that they should be tormented five months; and their torment was as the torment of a scorpion, when he striketh a man. And in those days shall men seek death, and shall not find it; and shall desire to die, and death shall flee from them.

If you do not have the seal of the Annunaki on your forehead, you are not going to enjoy those five months. If you believe that God is doing this, I feel sorry for you. I strongly suspect that Enlil has been planning for and orchestrating events to ensure that the Annunaki get their revenge upon mankind ever since they found out that some survived the flood. There may be absolutely nothing that we can do about that except hope that they change their minds, an extremely unlikely possibility. However, if mankind wakes up and realizes what the truth really is, we may be able to alter the horrible ordeals of the Great Tribulation.

I have already stated on several occasions that the Annunaki are much smarter than we are. In a strange sort of way, that fact is the only excuse that mankind has for believing the nonsense that we have been tricked, conned, and deceived into believing about the Bible. I do not believe that mankind is really so dumb that we would interpret the Bible as we have had we not been deceived and manipulated by far more intelligent beings. There is probably a great amount of mind control occurring as well. The verses quoted above from Revelation are another example of how we have been deceived into believing falsehoods. The verses describing the five months of torment mentioned above are simply an example of cruelty and total disregard for human life. The Great Tribulation must also be related in some way to the genetic engineering experiment. No father who is supreme would have any reason to mistreat his child like that. The Annunaki proved that they have no regard for human life when they took the vow to allow mankind to be totally wiped out by the flood. There is certainly no reason to believe that their attitude has changed.

It is just as nonsensical to believe that God would create a race of people in such a way that all of them are sinful, choose a few of them to spend eternity in paradise with him, and send the rest to a lake of fire. I have no doubt that the Annunaki have a lake of fire in their underground world; I also have no doubt that they have put plenty of slaves into it and will continue to do so. No just father would punish all his children for the disobedience of one; an all-knowing, heavenly father certainly would not. The Annunaki have done a masterful job of deceiving us and causing us to believe all sorts of nonsense. We must wake up before it is too late.

If mankind has any hopes of altering the Great Tribulation, I must discuss some scripture that is going to be very difficult for Christians; I have already discussed the Exodus, which I know was very difficult for the Jews. All mankind must join together and learn the truth. 1 John 4:2–3 says,

> Hereby know ye the Spirit of God: Every spirit
> that confesseth that Jesus Christ is come in the
> flesh is of God: And every spirit that confesseth

not that Jesus Christ is come in the flesh is not of
God: and this is that spirit of antichrist, whereof
ye have heard that it should come; and even now
already is it in the world.

Jesus Christ did come in the flesh. He is probably
the greatest of all those who were an offspring of a
son of god and daughter of man. The virgin birth was
probably the result of simply artificially inseminating a
young human with the DNA of one of the great gods of
the Annunaki. I believe that the sperm came from Enlil.
If we had the records and the knowledge to do such a
thing, I believe that we would find that the Virgin Mary
is blood related to Enlil. She was obviously not a half
sister, but I do believe that there was something very
special about her DNA.

It is unfortunate that the Bible does not give us
the genealogy of Mary; however, we are given the
genealogies of her husband, Joseph. The inerrant word
of God gives us two of them for Joseph, and they do not
agree. The first chapter of Matthew begins with one of
the genealogies of Joseph; this genealogy begins with
Abraham and goes through the generations until verse
16 says,

And Jacob begat Joseph the husband of Mary, of
whom was born Jesus, who is called Christ.

The other genealogy of Joseph is found in the third chapter of Luke; it says in verse 23,

> And Jesus himself began to be about thirty years of age, being (as was supposed) the son of Joseph, which was the son of Heli.

The genealogy of Joseph continues to be traced on back to Adam in verses 24–28 of Luke. Matthew says that Jacob was the father of Joseph; Luke says that Heli was the father of Joseph. There is something that smells very fishy going on here.

Matthew traces the genealogy of Joseph back to David through Solomon (David's son by Bathsheba). Luke traces the genealogy of Joseph back to David through Nathan (another of David's sons by Bathsheba and a brother of Solomon). The theologians will not discuss this discrepancy and obvious attempt at deception with me.

Another point that they will not discuss with me is that the Bible says that Jesus was not the son of Joseph, but Joseph was a descendent of David (whichever genealogy you choose). Therefore if Jesus is not a descendent of Joseph, he is also not a descendent of David (unless he is descended from David through his mother Mary). Mary's genealogy is never given, so why would anyone just assume that Jesus is a descendent of David, i.e., the Messiah? I believe that Jesus was chosen, just like

Abraham was, to fulfill a role in the masterful drama that the Annunaki are playing out. There is also something very special about his DNA.

Enki was on Earth when Jesus was born; he knew about the spiritual deception that Enlil had created for mankind. He was very aware that great powers would be given to Jesus by Enlil. He knew that great damage to mankind would result from the deception about Jesus. Enki used King Herod as a human proxy to try to kill Jesus. The fact that Herod wanted to kill the young Jesus is confirmed in Matthew 2:13:

> And when they were departed, behold, the angel of the Lord appeareth to Joseph in a dream, saying, Arise, and take the young child and his mother, and flee into Egypt, and be thou there until I bring thee word: for Herod will seek the young child to destroy him.

After Jesus had become an adult, Enki tried another ploy. The description of this is found in Matthew 4:1–11.

> Then Jesus was led up by the Spirit into the wilderness to be tempted by the devil. He fasted forty days and forty nights, and afterwards he was famished. The tempter came and said to him, "If

you are the Son of God, command these stones to become loaves of bread." But he answered, "It is written, One does not live by bread alone, but by every word that comes from the mouth of God." Then the devil took him to the holy city and placed him on the pinnacle of the temple, saying to him, "If you are the Son of God, throw yourself down; for it is written, "He will command his angels concerning you, and, On their hands they will bear you up, so that you will not dash your foot against a stone." Jesus said to him, "Again it is written, Do not put the Lord your God to the test." Again the devil took him to a very high mountain and showed him all the kingdoms of the world and their splendor; and he said to him, "All these I will give you, if you will fall down and worship me." Jesus said to him, "Away with you, Satan! for it is written, "Worship the Lord your God, and serve only him."

Jesus was not as easily deceived by the Annunaki as we have been. He resisted the temptations by Enki. Mankind would have been much better off if Enki had been successful. Enki, once again, was trying to salvage the spirituality of his creation.

I believe that Jesus is the son of Enlil. I believe that Jesus was guided and directed by Enlil from the time of his birth until the time of his crucifixion and resurrection, and I believe that Jesus sits at the right hand of Enlil on Nibiru today. I believe that Jesus will return to Earth; I believe that he will return during the Age of Pisces. We are currently in the Age of Pisces; it will end around AD 2100. I believe that Jesus will become King of Kings and Lord of Lords and rule Earth with an iron rod. The Revelation to St. John, chapter 19, verses 11–16 says,

> And I saw heaven opened, and behold a white horse; and he that sat upon him was called Faithful and True, and in righteousness he doth judge and make war. His eyes were as a flame of fire, and on his head were many crowns; and he had a name written, that no man knew, but he himself. And he was clothed with a vesture dipped in blood: and his name is called The Word of God. And the armies which were in heaven followed him upon white horses, clothed in fine linen, white and clean. And out of his mouth goeth a sharp sword, that with it he should smite the nations: and he shall rule them with a rod of iron: and he treadeth the winepress of the fierceness and wrath of Almighty God. And he hath on his vesture and on his thigh a name written, KING OF KINGS, AND LORD OF LORDS.

The Annunaki are very dramatic. They seem to love pomp, circumstance, and pageantry. However, I do not believe for one minute that the real God has any need to make war on anybody or that he has any need to try to impress anybody with pomp and pageantry. I do not believe that he would dip his clothes in blood, and I do not believe that he will rule with an iron rod.

I do believe that Jesus was resurrected from the dead; I do not know whether the resurrection actually occurred on day three following his crucifixion. In 1 Peter 3:18–19 in the Bible we find the following:

> For Christ also hath once suffered for sins, the just for the unjust, that he might bring us to God, being put to death in the flesh, but quickened by the Spirit: By which also he went and preached unto the spirits in prison.

I believe that Jesus was resurrected shortly after being entombed; it seems to me that the sooner after death that it was done, the easier it would be.

I believe that he was taken to the lower world, and he preached to the inhabitants there. The genetic experiment must certainly be going on underground as well as on the surface. The laboratory, if you will, must be underground; the databases and records must be kept underground as well. I believe that Jesus returned to the surface on day three and was seen by mankind again at that time.

The ancient texts describe several such resurrections from the dead; they also show pictures of the process. There is also evidence in the Bible that the same process that is described in the ancient texts was used to resurrect Jesus.

The ancient texts describe the use of the food of life and the water of life for the resurrection as well as the use of a pulsar and an emitter. I believe that the pulsar was a device like our defibrillator; it was used to shock the heart and restart it. I believe that the emitter released some sort of irradiation (the pictures in the ancient texts certainly suggest this).

The Bible says in John 20:17:

> Jesus saith unto her, Touch me not; for I am not
> yet ascended to my Father: but go to my brethren,
> and say unto them, I ascend unto my Father, and
> your Father; and to my God, and your God.

Jesus made this statement to Mary Magdalene when she was at his tomb shortly after his resurrection. Why would he not want her to touch him? I believe that the answer is that he was still radioactive from the emitter.

Who or what is the Antichrist? Antichrist as used in the Bible is easily understood if one simply remembers that the story of the Bible is the story of a family dispute between Enki and Enlil. Some human proxy representing Enki is the Antichrist; Enlil and his partly human proxy, Jesus, are the opponents. Scripture concerning the Antichrist is found in 2 Thessalonians 2:6–12:

> And now ye know what withholdeth that he might be revealed in his time. For the mystery of iniquity doth already work: only he who now letteth will let, until he be taken out of the way. And then shall that Wicked be revealed, whom the Lord shall consume with the spirit of his mouth, and shall destroy with the brightness of his coming: Even him, whose coming is after the working of Satan with all power and signs and lying wonders, And with all deceivableness of unrighteousness in them that perish; because they received not the love of the truth, that they might be saved. And for this cause God shall send them strong delusion, that they should believe a lie: That they all might be damned who believed not the truth, but had pleasure in unrighteousness.

The wicked that will be revealed is the human proxy of Enki; his coming is due to the influence of Enki. Enlil is saying that anyone who supports Enki will be sent a strong delusion and believe a lie. I think that the lie that people will believe is that the Antichrist is Jesus. Indeed, many slaves have been deluded into believing another lie, *the grandest deception.* I ask the reader, why would any heavenly father ever want to intentionally deceive his children and cause them to believe a lie of any kind? That is preposterous.

There has been a lot of speculation recently about the Mayan calendar ending December 21, 2012. I personally do not believe that anything of major significance will occur on that date. If the end of the world does occur on that date, so be it. We cannot do anything about that. The Annunaki were great stargazers. They knew more about the stars, the zodiac, astronomy, and astrology five hundred thousand years ago than we do now. Time is cyclical to both the Mayans and the Annunaki. The end of one age is the beginning of another. I am the alpha and omega. I am the beginning and the end. Perhaps the main reason that I do not think that anything of significance will happen on that date is that the Bible describes a lot of things that are supposed to happen after that date. I will make a wish about December 21, 2012. I hope that, by that date, enough people will have come to believe what I am saying in this little book that the governments, religions, and banking systems in our world will come to an end and be replaced with institutions that serve mankind.

The Annunaki nuked their spaceport in the Sinai Peninsula in 2024 BCE. The same son of Enki who married Ereshkigal and became lord of the lower world, Nergal, was the primary one responsible for the terrible act. Nergal had had a long-standing disagreement with his father; this disagreement led to Nergal siding with Enlil in the family feud. Ninurta, a son of Enlil, was Nergal's accomplice in the nuclear destruction. The two of them had convinced Enlil to give his permission for them to do the dastardly deed. They convinced Enlil that Marduk, a son of Enki, was going to take over control of the spaceport in the Sinai unless he was stopped. Rather than surrendering control of the spaceport to Enki, Enlil agreed to allow the boys to destroy it. Photographs taken from space still show the immense cavity and the crack in the surface where the nuclear explosion occurred. The area is still strewn with crushed, burnt, and blackened rocks. These rocks have a highly unusual ratio of the uranium 235 isotope. The experts say that this indicates sudden, immense heat of nuclear origin.

Nergal lived in his subterranean paradise with Ereshkigal. He came to the surface to nuke the spaceport. The ancient tablets make it clear that the deed was done from an airplane of some sort. When they come to the surface today to engage in some activity, we call the airplane an unidentified flying object.

It seems to me that if the Mayans are correct, the inerrant word of God would mention their prediction. It also seems to me that it would mention a nuclear disaster of the magnitude of the one in the Sinai Peninsula or the ones at Nagasaki and Hiroshima. No mention of any of these events can be found in the Bible.

Chapter 8

ARMAGEDDON

I believe that Armageddon is the place, Har-Megiddo at the foot of Mount Megiddo, where a war will take place during the Age of Pisces. The war at Armageddon is actually good news in one way; mankind realizes that something is not right in our world. At least they realize that the Israelites are not God's chosen people. However, the nation of Israel must have become a very powerful nation by that time. All the other nations join forces against Israel for the battle at Armageddon.

Concerning a great battle that is to be fought in the future, we find in Revelation 16:16.

> And he gathered them together into a place called in the Hebrew tongue Armageddon.

At this time, Jesus returns and harvests the Earth; he is trying to find support for Israel (Enlil) for this war. He finds none (mankind has realized that they have been deceived about Israel and about Jesus). In Isaiah 63:3–4, Jesus says,

> I have trodden the winepress alone, and of the people there was none with me: for I will tread them in mine anger, and trample them in my fury; and their blood shall be sprinkled upon my garments, and I will stain all my raiment. For the day of vengeance is in mine heart, and the year of my redeemed is come.

Jesus finds no support for Israel; sadly, Jesus too has been deceived by Enlil. Jesus is extremely angry; he seeks revenge for all the things that mankind has done to him. Jesus is actually a very tragic figure in the drama orchestrated by Enlil. He was deceived into believing that Enlil was God, he was terribly abused and mistreated during his life on Earth, and he has been turned into an angry, vengeful monster by Enlil.

There are many parallels between the twenty-first-century BCE and the twenty-first-century AD. Nuclear weapons may be used at some point during the next ninety years as they were in the twenty-first-century BCE. But I do not think that the battle at Armageddon will be fought until around AD 2160, and we can hope that it will not be nuclear.

I believe that the battle at Armageddon and what is referred to as the second coming of Christ will occur around that time because the Bible says in Daniel 12:5–7 concerning these things,

> Then I Daniel looked, and, behold, there stood other two, the one on this side of the bank of the river, and the other on that side of the bank of the river. And one said to the man clothed in linen, which was upon the waters of the river, How long shall it be to the end of these wonders? And I heard the man clothed in linen, which was upon the waters of the river, when he held up his right hand and his left hand unto heaven, and sware by him that liveth for ever that it shall be for a time, times, and an half; and when he shall have accomplished to scatter the power of the holy people, all these things shall be finished.

Daniel is being told by Michael and two other emissaries of Enlil that all these things shall be finished in a time, times and an half. I believe that this is saying that the Old World Order, if I may call it that, of things will be finished in a time, times, and a half a time. The time span begins when the daily sacrifice at the temple in Jerusalem is abolished.

The daily sacrifice was abolished by Antiochus Epiphanes; this is found in Daniel 8:11–12:

> Yea, he magnified himself even to the prince of the host, and by him the daily sacrifice was taken away, and the place of his sanctuary was cast down. And an host was given him against the daily sacrifice by reason of transgression, and it cast down the truth to the ground; and it practiced, and prospered.

Antiochus Epiphanes became the king of Greece in 175 BCE; he plundered the temple in Jerusalem and desecrated it by offering pig's flesh on the altar. He ended the daily sacrifices and ceremonies about 171 BCE.

My guess is that the time, times, and half a time refer to the number of the beast or man's number, 666. Therefore, $666 + 2 \times 666 + 333 = 2{,}333$. So 2333—171 = AD 2161.

We find this same usage of words in Revelation 12:13–14:

> And when the dragon saw that he had been cast unto the earth, he persecuted the woman which brought forth the man child. And to the woman

were given two wings of a great eagle, that she
might fly into the wilderness, into her place,
where she is nourished for a time, and times,
and half a time.

The dragon, of course, is Enki. The supporters of
Enki include anyone who opposes Enlil. The woman is
Israel, the supporters of Enlil (whether they know it or
not). This just says that Israel will be protected until the
New World Order can be established and that that will
happen in a time, times, and half a time. Again, that will
be from 171 BCE until about AD 2161.

The only other time the phrase is used in the Bible, to
my knowledge, is in Daniel 7:25:

And he shall speak great words against the most
High, and shall wear out the saints of the most
High, and think to change times and laws: and
they shall be given into his hand until a time and
times and the dividing of time.

Again, it was Antiochus Epiphanes who attempted to
change times and laws by abolishing the daily sacrifice.
The persecution of the Jews by Antiochus Epiphanes
lasted for 2,300 days (from 171 BCE until December 25,
165 BCE). I think that all this says that Jesus will return,
make preparations for the war at Armageddon, win that

war, and establish a New World Order by around AD 2160. That is close enough for me.

In the Dead Sea Scrolls found at Qumran and the adjacent caves mention of this war is also found. The Essenes describe this war in one of the longest and most complete scrolls that has been found. This scroll is titled by scholars *The War of the Sons of Light Against the Sons of Darkness.* Although, it seems that Enki is Lucifer (carrier of light) in the Bible, I believe that the Enlilites are the Sons of Light and that the Enkiites are the Sons of Darkness. Enlil, when the lots were cast, was given authority over the upper world (aboveground, light) and Enki was given authority over the lower world (underground, darkness). Of course, the Enlilites also represent the good guys and the Enkiites represent the bad guys in the biblical version of the battle. Since the Enlilites win the war, Enki must pay a penalty. He must not leave the underground or influence either Jesus or the humans in any way for one thousand years. The biblical verses describing this penalty are found in Revelation 20:2–3:

> And he laid hold on the dragon, that old serpent, which is the Devil, and Satan, and bound him a thousand years, And cast him into the bottomless pit, and shut him up, and set a seal upon him, that he should deceive the nations no more, til the thousand years should be fulfilled: and after that he must be loosed a little season.

If the script written by the Enlilites becomes fact, Jesus will judge mankind at that time and determine which slaves have supported Enlil and which slaves have supported Enki. The Bible refers to this as the sheep-goat judgment found in Matthew 25:31–33:

> When the Son of man shall come in his glory, and all the holy angels with him, then shall he sit upon the throne of his glory: And before him shall be gathered all nations: and he shall separate them one from another, as a shepherd divideth his sheep from the goats: And he shall set the sheep on his right hand, but the goats on the left.

The slaves who supported Enlil (Israel) will be deemed sheep; the slaves who supported Enki will be deemed goats. The goats will be thrown into the bottomless pit in the lower world. There will be weeping and gnashing of teeth.

The humans who refused to participate in the family feud will regroup under a New World Order. Some of them will have to rebuild Jerusalem, Israel, and anything else the Enlilites want rebuilt. Jerusalem will, once again, become mission control center.

Do you find it interesting that mankind is now being referred to as sheep and goats (lowly animals)? What happened to "the children of God"? The Annunaki have no more concern for human life than we do for the lives of cockroaches (I should have said laboratory rats). If there is any doubt in your mind about what value the Annunaki place on human life, let me quote what they have to say about that from Isaiah 2:22:

> Cease ye from man, whose breath is in his nostrils:
> for wherein is he to be accounted of?

This verse is supposed to be God speaking (it is really Enlil speaking); the verse says that because mankind has such a short life span (his breath is in his nostrils) he is of no value. Indeed, in Annunaki years, we are of little value individually. If one works for them for sixty Earth years (a very long time to work in human terms), that amounts to 60/3600 of an Annunaki year (or about six days in Annunaki terms). As individuals, we are only laboratory animals to the Annunaki.

There are some verses in the Bible that I hope that every reader of this book will take the time to look at and ponder over. They are found in Revelation 10:8–10 and are about the little book. I feel certain that the little book is the Bible. John wrote the following:

> And the voice which I heard from heaven spake
> unto me again, and said, Go and take the little
> book which is open in the hand of the angel
> which standeth upon the sea and upon the

> earth. And I went unto the angel, and said unto
> him, Give me the little book. And he said unto me,
> Take it, and eat it up; and it shall make thy belly
> bitter, but it shall be in thy mouth sweet as honey.

When we first read the Bible, it is, indeed, as sweet as honey. We are told that we are a child of God, that he loves us, and that if we obey his instructions, there is a good chance that we will spend eternity with him in paradise. When we have digested it and begin to understand what it really says, it makes my stomach quite bitter. I repeat, it is a travesty of deception.

If any slaves are resurrected from the dead or "raptured," it will be ones with very close bloodlines to Enlil. No supporters or descendents of Enki will be resurrected. DNA might be taken and the person essentially cloned, thus resurrected. They may resurrect some in other ways as well. In regard to resurrection of the dead, the Bible states in Colossians 1:18:

> And he is the head of the body, the church; who is
> the beginning, the firstborn from the dead; that
> in all things he might have the preeminence.

The Christian theologians speak endlessly about this resurrection; I have never heard a single one of them speak about all the other people who were resurrected from the dead when Jesus was crucified. I have read that as many as five hundred other people may have been resurrected on this occasion. I have not been able to find a single preacher or priest who was willing to even discuss the matter with me. I refer to Matthew 27:50–53:

> Jesus, when he had cried again with a loud voice, yielded up the ghost. And, behold, the veil of the temple was rent in twain from the top to the bottom; and the earth did quake, and the rocks rent; And the graves were opened; and many bodies of the saints which slept arose, And came out of the graves after his resurrection, and went into the holy city, and appeared unto many.

Again, this is very confusing, i.e., (1) the verse in Colossians says that Jesus was the firstborn resurrected from the dead; the verse in Matthew seems to say that when Jesus died, some arose and came out of their graves; and (2) Jesus was supposed to have been resurrected on day three following his crucifixion; were these others resurrected before or after he was, or (3) were the graves just opened and no one resurrected for three days? Why the deception? Who were these who were resurrected? Do they ever die again? Are they with us today? Are they descendents of the Annunaki? Do they run the world today? I believe that they were Annunaki.

In November of 2005 some archaeologists found the oldest Christian church ever found in Israel. Inscriptions in Greek suggest that it was built or rebuilt in the third-century AD. After careful excavation, the center of a magnificent mosaic floor depicting two fishes came into view. Two fishes are the zodiacal sign of Pisces. This church was found at the foot of Mount Megiddo, Har-Megiddo, Armageddon. I do not know when exactly, but I do believe that the battle will take place there during the Age of Pisces.

After the slaves rebuild the homeland of the Annunaki, Israel, Jesus will reign there for one thousand years. He will impose the conditions of the New World Order and he will rule with an iron rod. There will be peace during those years; Jesus is so ruthless that no one will dare oppose him. The bottom line on the battle at Armageddon is that Jesus has returned and set up a New World Order.

The good news is that mankind has a chance to grow spiritually because Jesus and the Bible have been exposed. Unfortunately for mankind, the living conditions imposed by Jesus under the New World Order will be very severe.

Chapter 9

THE AGE OF AQUARIUS

The Age of Aquarius begins around AD 2100. It may even begin in AD 2160. If the one-thousand-year reign of Jesus begins in AD 2161, it would end in AD 3161. At any rate, the battle at Armageddon has been fought. Jesus is nearing the end of his one-thousand-year reign. There is peace on earth. However, Enki is nearing the end of his sentence as well. When one thinks of time in terms of Annunaki life spans, I find it very interesting that Jesus (part human) is given authority for such a short time, i.e., one thousand years. By the same token, Enki (all Annunaki) is given a very short sentence, i.e., one thousand years. We are given some information about what happens during the Age of Aquarius in Revelation 20:7–9:

> And when the thousand years are expired, Satan
> shall be loosed out of his prison, And shall go out
> to deceive the nations that are in the four quarters
> of the earth, Gog and Magog, to gather them
> together to battle: the number of whom is as the
> sand of the sea. And they went up the breadth of
> the earth, and compassed the camp of the saints
> about, and the beloved city: and fire came down
> from God out of heaven, and devoured them.

After the thousand years, Enki is free to influence mankind once again. Mankind has finally seen the light. They have suffered greatly under the iron rod of Jesus for one thousand years. Almost all humans now realize that Jesus is not God (the number of whom is as the sand of the sea). They are angry. They want revenge for all the atrocities that Jesus and the Annunaki have heaped upon them. Enki organizes them for battle against Jerusalem (the beloved city).

Before I continue, allow me to reveal to you what life is like for mankind under the iron rod of Jesus. It is described in Zechariah 14:14–19:

> And Judah also shall fight at Jerusalem; and the
> wealth of all the heathen round about shall be
> gathered together, gold and silver, and apparel,
> in great abundance. And so shall be the plague

of the horse, of the mule, of the camel, and of the ass, and of all the beasts that shall be in these tents, as this plague. And it shall come to pass, that every one that is left of all the nations which came against Jerusalem shall even go up from year to year to worship the King, the Lord of hosts, and to keep the feast of tabernacles. And it shall be, that whoso will not come up of all the families of the earth unto Jerusalem to worship the King, the Lord of hosts, even upon them shall be no rain. And if the family of Egypt go not up, and come not, that have no rain; there shall be the plague, wherewith the Lord will smite the heathen that come not up to keep the feast of tabernacles. This shall be the punishment of Egypt, and the punishment of all nations that come not up to keep the feast of tabernacles.

These verses say that every nation on Earth will have to bring gold, silver, and clothing in great abundance to Jerusalem and give it to Jesus. The world has been devastated by a world war; in spite of this, if mankind has anything of value (horse, mule, camel, anything) it will have to be brought to Jerusalem and given to Jesus.

We think that our taxes are way too high, and they are. Our burden today is nothing compared to the hardships that the iron rod of Jesus is going to impose on mankind. Everything will be in short supply (food, medicine, all necessities of life); nevertheless, every year representatives from every nation will have to travel to Jerusalem and give Jesus anything they might have of value. If the representatives from any nation fail to do so, there will be no rain in that nation for the following year. If the representatives from that nation still refuse to go to Jerusalem, the next year a plague will be sent to that nation. There is probably no way that anyone would survive both the drought and the plague. Jesus has apparently remembered every lash and wound that he suffered at the hands of man; he shows no mercy during the one thousand years of his reign.

By the way, the feast of tabernacles was a yearly occurrence for the Israelites in the Old Testament. It was a weeklong celebration. They were required to bring gifts and sacrifices to the temple that were over and above all the other gifts and sacrifices they had given all year long. They had to live in booths during this festival. It created quite a hardship. Unfortunately, mankind has realized the truth too late. "Fire came down from heaven and devoured them." I will address that later.

The Annunaki have made an attempt to accumulate everything of value on planet Earth. They are ready for the return of their home planet. The year is approximately AD 3400. Nibiru approaches Earth. Speaking of some

future return of God (really Nibiru), we find in Isaiah
13:13:

> Therefore I will shake the heavens, and the earth
> shall remove out of her place, in the wrath of the
> Lord of hosts, and in the day of his fierce anger.

The lord of hosts mentioned above is not a vengeful
Supreme Being wreaking havoc on mankind because he
is angry. The lord of hosts mentioned above is the planet
Nibiru. The planet is also called *god* and the lord of hosts
in the creation epic. Nibiru passes close enough to Earth
for Earth to be shaken in such a way that some sort of
natural disaster almost completely destroys human life
on this planet.

Perhaps a moon or other satellite of Nibiru actually
hits Earth. That would be a repeat performance of what
occurred when a moon of Nibiru struck Tiamat, creating
Earth and the asteroid belt some 4.5 billion years ago;
the end result is just different. The psalmist who wrote
the eighty-second psalm did say, if you recall, that
"the foundations of the earth are out of course." The
consequences of this natural disaster are referred to in
Isaiah 13:12:

> I will make man more precious than fine gold;
> even a man than the golden wedge of Ophir.

What is being said is that mankind will be so entirely wiped out by this event that a man will become more precious than fine gold. A man will be as rare as the gold at Ophir, following the event. Ophir is believed to be a place in Africa, possibly Rhodesia, where the Annunaki found a lot of gold. Gold mines found in Africa have been dated to be over two hundred thousand years old. The Annunaki apparently mined them at Ophir until only minute traces of gold remained.

We find further confirmation of this decimation of mankind in Isaiah 24:6:

> Therefore hath the curse devoured the earth, and they that dwell therein are desolate: therefore the inhabitants of the earth are burned, and few men left.

The Annunaki know that the natural disaster will occur when Nibiru returns on one of its orbits, just as they knew that the flood would occur when Nibiru approached near Earth about thirteen thousand years ago. They plan to use this disaster to help them annihilate mankind again. I believe that this will occur when Nibiru next returns around AD 3400.

I am not going to take the time to quote the entire chapter, but one description of this natural disaster and the concomitant slaughter of mankind by the Annunaki can be found in the thirteenth chapter of Isaiah. I will just supply a few of the highlights:

> Howl ye; for the day of the Lord is at hand; it shall come as a destruction from the Almighty . . . they shall be afraid—they shall be in pain—they shall be amazed one at another; their faces shall be as flames—the stars of heaven and the constellations thereof shall not give their light: the sun shall be darkened in his going forth, and the moon shall not cause her light to shine—I will shake the heavens, and the earth shall remove out of her place—Every one that is found shall be thrust through; and every one that is joined unto them shall fall by the sword. Their children also shall be dashed to pieces before their eyes; their houses shall be spoiled, and their wives ravished.

If you believe that those are the actions of God, there is no hope for you. Please close this book, and do not read any farther. You have been dumbed down to the point that you cannot be repaired.

All mankind has now realized that the stories about the Bible that were ingrained into their little minds as children are not true. Enki has organized them for battle in order to get their revenge; the natural disaster thwarts their efforts. There are other verses in Isaiah about this natural disaster that are even more hideous than the ones described above. I think that one example of that is enough, however.

Isaiah was prophesying around 700 BCE. Nibiru passed through our vicinity about 200 BCE. The next orbit will probably be the one that causes the disaster. The Annunaki would certainly be able to determine the exact path of Nibiru one orbit in advance. Astronomers today would know one year in advance if a large celestial body was on a collision course with Earth (I hope). The prophecy of Isaiah is not divinely inspired.

The Annunaki will use the natural disaster to try to rid the earth of all humans. They will slaughter as many survivors of this disaster as they can find. I believe that the Annunaki are so determined to rid Earth of mankind that even Jesus will be a casualty from this disaster. They do not want to leave any evidence of their genetic experiment behind. Would the Annunaki rid Earth of mankind so that the inhabitants of Nibiru can live here?

Is it possible that the passage of Nibiru disturbs the asteroid belt ("I will shake the heavens") in such a way that Earth is hit by such a large asteroid that Earth's orbit is altered ("the earth shall remove out of her place")? If so, that would certainly cause a disaster that would kill most of mankind.

In the Revelation of St. John, we find the following in verses 1–3:

> And I saw a new heaven and a new earth: for the first heaven and the first earth were passed away; and there was no more sea. And I John saw the holy city, new Jerusalem, coming down from God out of heaven, prepared as a bride adorned for her husband." And I heard a great voice out of heaven saying, Behold the tabernacle of God is with men, and he will dwell with them, and they shall be his people, and God himself, shall be with them, and be their God.

If the above scenario is correct, the asteroid belt and Earth would certainly be altered (passed away). Sea, at times, in the Bible refers to multitudes, nations, and/ or people. No more sea could mean that mankind is totally eliminated. It could also mean that Earth is totally destroyed.

What and where are the new heaven, the new earth, and the New Jerusalem? I assume that parts of the asteroid belt survive. That could be the new heaven, or the new heaven may be the asteroids that are formed from the destruction of Earth. The new Earth may be what survives from the old Earth; it could also be Nibiru.

John says he saw New Jerusalem coming down from God (Nibiru). I believe that there are also two possibilities here. If Earth survives, New Jerusalem will be built on Earth. If that is the case, I believe that the Annunaki will abandon Nibiru and make Earth their new home. If Earth does not survive, New Jerusalem is on Nibiru. If New Jerusalem is on Nibiru, it is probably already built and the home of the Annunaki.

The description of New Jerusalem begins in verses 10–12 of the twenty-first chapter of the Revelation:

> And he carried me away in the spirit to a great and high mountain, and showed me that great city, the holy Jerusalem, descending out of heaven from God, Having the glory of God: and her light was like unto a stone most precious, even like a jasper stone, clear as crystal; And had a wall great and high, and had twelve gates, and at the gates twelve angels, and names written thereon, which were the names of the twelve tribes of the children of Israel.

The light of New Jerusalem seems to come from the gemstone jasper (not sunlight). The underground light of the mind-controlling machine mentioned earlier was also produced by gold and yellow diamonds. The description continues in verses 16–18:

> And the city lieth foursquare, and the length is
> as large as the breadth: and he measured the
> city with the reed, twelve thousand furlongs.
> The length and the breadth and the height of it
> are equal. And he measured the wall thereof, an
> hundred and forty and four cubits, according to
> the measure of a man, that is, of the angel. And
> the building of the wall of it was of jasper; and
> the city was pure gold, like unto clear glass.

The city is in the shape of a cube. Each side of the cube is 12,000 furlongs or 1,500 miles long. Each wall is 144 cubits or 216 feet thick. That is huge; no light can penetrate this structure, verse 23 continues,

> And the city had no need of the sun, neither of
> the moon, to shine in it: for the glory of God did
> lighten it, and the lamb is the light thereof.

The longevity problem may not have been solved on Earth, or the Annunaki may just prefer to live underground (since they probably evolved there). New Jerusalem is underground. It may already exist on Nibiru. It may already be under construction on Earth. Either way, it is so large that I would bet that every Annunaki on Nibiru can live there. We now know why the Annunaki are so interested in obtaining gold, "and the city was pure gold."

The verses above say that God will dwell with men. One might ask who these men are. I believe that the Annunaki will still want slaves to do the work on the new earth and in New Jerusalem. I also believe that by that time, they will have progressed with their genetic engineering experiments to the point that they have perfected the process of making slaves. The slaves will be transported, raptured if you prefer, to New Jerusalem.

What will that slave be? I think that we find out in Revelation 21:4:

> And God shall wipe away all tears from their eyes; and there shall be no more death, neither sorrow, nor crying, neither shall there be any more pain: for the former things are passed away.

The perfected slave will not cry (or laugh). They will have longevity and will be allowed to eat the food of life and drink the water of life. They will have no emotions of any sort, such as sorrow (or happiness). They will have no feelings such as pain (or pleasure). There will be no marriage, no sex, no family, and no reproductive capability whatsoever. The dumbing-down process has been perfected. Mental activities of the slaves will be minimal. They are biological robots. They will not become noisy or boisterous. Enlil wins!

Chapter 10

WHAT DO WE DO NOW?

With the help of the Annunaki, we have made tremendous cultural and technological advances since the flood. We would not even exist had Enki chosen to keep his vow. I am grateful that I have had almost seventy years of existence on this planet. Even though I have been a slave for every one of those years, I have had my bright moments. I must admit, however, that I would have much preferred to have been a son of Anu, Enki, or Enlil. In spite of our advances, the Annunaki remain far ahead of us and superior to us in every way. We cannot compete with them. At this point, they still need us. We certainly need them. They still need the slaves to do the work that they do not want to do. They still need the laboratory animals to complete their experiment.

We need the use of their advanced technology and their guidance.

As for me, one lifetime of being a slave is enough. I am quite willing to undergo whatever destiny the Supreme Entity has for me. I would not want to be an Annunaki slave again even if I could live as one for another million years. I know of a way that the fate of mankind might be altered. Minds far more intelligent than mine will be required if Earth is to avoid the great natural disaster; however, there may be a way that mankind can survive it. I cannot delineate the details for such plans in this book for obvious reasons. In order for such a plan to become reality, humans will have to become (just as Woodrow Wilson said of the Annunaki) so organized, so subtle, so watchful, so interlocked, so complete, and so pervasive that we can compete with them. I am going to invite anyone who has an interest in exploring such possibilities to contact me; also, feel free to contact me if you would like to discuss any aspect of this book or related topic. You will find an invitation and a way to contact me at the end of the book.

If I may be so bold, I would like to give some advice to the Annunaki. First and most importantly, find a way to live at peace with each other. Love your brother as you have advised us to do. Find a better way to settle your disputes. If the natural disaster cannot be avoided, help mankind survive it. Be open and honest with us. When dealing with us, please make any instructions perfectly clear. Remember that you are far more intelligent than we are. What may seem perfectly clear to you may be extremely confusing to us. You are far superior to us in every way. We pose no threat to you. We will never catch up no matter how much you help us. If you want us to work for you, pay us an honest wage, and we will do so, but allow us to be free. Let us evolve into whatever we may become instead of keeping us dumbed down and in servitude to you. Help us with our medical problems so that we can live longer, healthier lives. Teach us how to restore our planet and turn it into a Garden of Eden.

I also have some advice for my fellow man. Do not be discouraged. Enlil may succeed in turning mankind into a biological robot. Life will go on. I believe that time is cyclical. I believe that the end of one age is the beginning of another. The destiny of mankind will not be determined by Enlil. Mankind's destiny, just like yours, mine, and Enlil's will be determined by a power far greater than any of us. Enjoy your life. Learn how to be calm and peaceful. Love your fellow man.

Mankind has absolutely no hopes of ever becoming anything other than dumbed-down slaves unless we do at least three things. First, we must control our own money system; the Federal Reserve banking system must be eliminated. We kicked them out once under President Andrew Jackson, eliminated the national debt, and the citizenry were, in general, quite prosperous. We must kick them out again. Second, the government must be answerable to the public, and the citizenry must find a way to get honest information from the government. Third, mankind must realize that all religions on this planet are harmful to their well-being and spiritual growth. We must not let ourselves be deceived by false doctrine regardless of what our itching ears want to hear. Do not get me wrong; I do believe that there is a Supreme Entity of some sort. As of today, that entity has not chosen to write an instruction book. Well, the instruction book may have been written; if so, no one has been able to read it as yet. Even the great Annunaki cannot read it. I must find time to research that further; then, perhaps, I will write another book.

Chapter 11

WHO, WHAT, AND WHERE IS GOD?

I am not trying to tell anyone who, what, or where God is. I am just going to share some ideas with you about my beliefs. I believe that God is *all.* He is all-inclusive. He is all matter, all energy, and all spirit that exists.

I do believe that the big bang theory is correct. I believe that the small speck that exploded to create our universe was God. He is everything that is in this universe. You, me, and everything that is in this universe are part of him; that makes each individual and everything in the universe important since it is part of God. We should treat all that is in this universe accordingly.

I also believe that there may have been other big bangs before this one; I believe that there will be others after this one. Our universe is expanding. I believe that a time will come when the universe stops expanding and implodes back upon itself. All matter, all energy, and every particle will coalesce into a pinpoint speck again. Another big bang will occur.

Each big bang is different; God expresses himself differently each time a new big bang occurs. After all, he does not want to get bored. This process will repeat itself endlessly for all eternity.

Our spirit, or soul, will also exist for all eternity. Enjoy your life. Treat everything and everybody as though they were a part of God because they are. It is quite a journey.

Part 2:
The Grandest
Rebellion

Chapter 1

NOW I KNOW

I realize that part 1 of this book is a hard read because the material is so new and foreign to most people. Please forgive me for being somewhat repetitious in this first chapter of part 2. I thought some repetition might be helpful in order to get some of the facts straight.

I was taught as a child that the Bible is the inerrant word of God. I was also taught that Jesus Christ was the Son of God and that if I believed in Jesus, I would be saved and live in paradise with God and Jesus for all eternity. I was taught that the Bible is an instruction book and that I should live my life according to the principles described in the book. I was baptized when I was ten years old; I came to believe as much as anyone ever has that what I had been taught as a child was the absolute truth.

When I began to experience the difficulties of life as a young man, I decided that I had better read the instruction book. After reading the Bible three or four times from cover to cover, I was very perplexed to realize that I could not understand the instruction book. I began to ask everyone who I thought might have some knowledge of the book what certain verses meant. I soon realized that no one knew what the book said, or at least, no one agreed about what it said.

I began to attend many different churches of different denominations. I asked people from each of these congregations what certain verses meant. I asked preachers, priests, rabbis, and various other theologians what certain verses meant. No two answers were ever the same. I attended various Bible study classes with the same results. Eventually, I heard that newer translations had been written; I had always read the King James Version. I bought a New International Version. I thought that this is wonderful; I can understand the English much easier. It was written in plain, simple English. I knew what practically every word in the book meant; I looked up the meanings of the others in the dictionary. I then knew the meaning of every word. However, the meaning of some verses remained unclear; some were nonsensical, and some contradicted another verse. Sum bitch! What is going on?

I bought every other translation that I could find; I compared verse to verse. I bought a Greek to English dictionary. I bought a Hebrew to English dictionary. I bought a Qur'an (Koran). I bought a Hebrew Bible. I bought a book of Mormon. Guess what? No two Bibles agree about what the inerrant word of God says. So which Bible is supposed to be the inerrant word of God? I spent many years going through this process. I thought that it was very strange that God would give an instruction book to his children that they could not understand; I also eventually realized that the Bible actually causes discord among people because they disagree about what it says. I knew that God would not write an instruction book for his children that would create discord.

One night while listening to a radio talk show, I heard about a book entitled *The 12th Planet* by Zecharia Sitchen. It sounded kind of interesting, so I bought a copy. I read the book, was intrigued by it, and read eight other books he has written about ancient tablets found in the lands of the Bible. I began to study these books and others related to them. I began to study the Dead Sea Scrolls and related materials. This study took many years as well, but now I know what the Bible says. You will too if you read the rest of this book.

We know that a race of beings called Annunaki came to Earth about 450,000 years ago. They came to Earth from a planet called Nibiru; this planet orbits our sun in a long elliptical orbit that takes approximately 3,600 years to complete (3,600 Earth years are equivalent to one Nibirian year). Because of this, the Annunaki have very long life spans compared to humans. My best guess is that a normal life span for an Annunaki is approximately 500,000 Earth years. These ancient astronauts had come to Earth in search of gold. They created mankind in their own image and likeness. Mankind was first used to do the laborious task of mining the gold. Eventually, some of the slaves were transferred to the Garden of Eden to till the garden and serve the Annunaki as house servants.

Mankind was later given the ability to reproduce, and they began to do so at a fairly rapid rate. They became too noisy and boisterous to suit the leader of the Annunaki who was named Enlil. About thirteen thousand years ago, the Annunaki were aware that a huge natural disaster was going to occur on Earth. The disaster was a flood that engulfed the entire planet. Enlil decided to use this disaster as a means to rid Earth of the bothersome humans. He encouraged the Annunaki to take a vow not to save any of the humans from the flood. All the Annunaki took this vow. However, things did not work out as Enlil had planned.

Enlil had a half brother named Enki. Their father was named Anu; he was the ruler of Nibiru. The boys had separate mothers. The maternal sides of the families had been engaged in a long-standing dispute on Nibiru over which son would succeed Anu as ruler. Enki decided to inform one of the slaves named Ziusudra (the biblical

Noah) about the flood. He taught Noah how to build a submarine and how to survive the flood.

The family of Noah and a navigator who had been provided by Enki survived the flood. The Annunaki had observed the catastrophe from Earth orbit. When the Annunaki returned to Earth after the waters had subsided, Enlil was infuriated to discover that some humans had survived. Enlil realized that Enki had broken his vow to not save the humans; Enlil was determined to get his revenge for the betrayal by his half brother. The long-standing feud between the half brothers was intensified because of this occurrence. The Bible is a story about the Annunaki, about the family dispute between these two half brothers, and about the fate of their creation, mankind.

The Annunaki have deceived mankind about the proper interpretation of the Bible. Everywhere that the word *God* is used in the Christian Bible or *Elohim* or *Yahweh* is used in the Hebrew Bible, one should substitute for it the word *Annunaki*. The truth concerning the Bible would then be much easier to understand. The Annunaki created various religions on Earth. They have used the different belief systems that they have instilled into mankind as a way to keep us constantly at odds with each other. Now that we know that, it is time to do something about it. Enlil decided to deceive mankind into believing in a monotheistic deity so that mankind would worship the Annunaki as well as work for them. Enki agreed that mankind should work for the Annunaki, but because mankind was created in a way that they were given a soul, Enki knew that mankind should not be deceived into worshiping the Annunaki.

Enki founded the Brotherhood of the Serpent, which was a secret society in ancient times. The Brotherhood was dedicated to the dissemination of spiritual knowledge and the attainment of spirituality for all spiritual beings, including humans. The Brotherhood was very influential in ancient times. Unfortunately, Enlil was able to take the leadership of the Brotherhood away from Enki. Enlil then turned the Brotherhood into a secret organization that would be used to repress the spirituality of mankind. All secret societies have evolved from the Brotherhood; they have had a chilling amount of success. They have created spiritual decay, unremitting physical hardships, poverty, and suppression of truth and knowledge for mankind.

The secret societies have managed to keep mankind impoverished and engaged in constant wars. Having mankind constantly engaged in warfare has greatly benefited the Annunaki agenda in several ways. One obvious benefit for the Annunaki is that humans are killed, thus limiting the population on Earth. Another benefit is that the Annunaki make huge sums of money from the wars since they own the majority of the companies that make the materials needed for wars. Wars never solve a problem; they just succeed in breeding more hatred and animosity between the parties involved. That in turn makes it easier to convince mankind to engage in another war. Mankind's attention and focus remains on each other; it should be on the Annunaki and what they are doing to us.

The intent of the Annunaki is to acquire all the gold on Earth as well as everything else of value on this planet. They have succeeded in acquiring much of it already. As long as mankind's attention can be kept focused on each other, the Annunaki will continue to acquire wealth relatively easily. We must put a halt to this.

The Annunaki have established an international banking system based on artificially produced cycles of inflation and deflation. This is one of the most hideous contrivances ever placed on mankind. It has guaranteed that the Annunaki become wealthier and mankind poorer with the passage of time. We call the branch of this international organization that operates in the USA the Federal Reserve Bank. The creation of fiat currency or funny money, as some like to call it, did not begin with the Federal Reserve Bank of the United States. This nefarious banking system has been in place for hundreds of years and is international in scope.

The banking system that most nations use today has now become a central banking network that can be coordinated from a single fixed location. If one is interested in how this all came about, I would suggest reading *Tragedy & Hope: A History of the World in Our Time* by the late Dr. Carroll Quigley. The secret societies that arose from the Brotherhood of the Serpent have been used to organize and coordinate this very corrupt international monetary system. The Annunaki and their descendents control the money system for the entire world.

The Federal Reserve Bank is a private, profit-driven corporation. Its sole purpose is to make money for the stockholders of the corporation. These money vultures have absolutely no concern for the welfare of the American people or the welfare of this nation. When talking about privately owned, central banks who loan money to governments, Napoleon Bonaparte said,

> The hand that gives is above the hand that takes. Money has no motherland; financiers are without patriotism and without decency: their sole object is gain.

Our Federal Reserve Bank is no different than any other central bank. If the United States of America is going to survive as a nation, we must eliminate this bank and control our own money. If mankind is going to survive as a race of beings, they must do likewise.

The Annunaki plan to create what they call a New World Order. This is a new system that consists of a single government that rules the entire world. This one world government will be headed by a ruthless dictator. His name is Jesus. He will rule with an iron rod. He will create extreme hardship on mankind. Poverty will be the norm. Everything that mankind possesses that is valuable will have to be given to the Annunaki. One of the descriptions of the New World Order can be found in Ezekiel 43:18–27:

> And he said unto me, Son of man, thus saith the Lord God; These are the ordinances of the altar in the day when they shall make it, to offer burnt offerings thereon, and to sprinkle blood thereon. And thou shalt give to the priests the Levites that be of the seed of Zadok, which approach unto me, saith the Lord God, a young bullock for a sin offering. And thou shalt take of the blood thereof, and put it on the four horns of it, and on the four corners of the settle, and upon the border round about: thus shalt thou cleanse and purge it. Thou shalt take the bullock also of the sin offering, and he shall burn it in the appointed place of the house, without the sanctuary. And on the second day thou shalt offer a kid of the goats without blemish for a sin offering; and they shall cleanse the altar, as they did cleanse it with the bullock. When thou hast made an end of cleansing it, thou shalt offer a

young bullock without blemish, and a ram out of the flock without blemish. And thou shalt offer them before the Lord, and the priests shalt cast salt upon them, and they shalt offer them up for a burnt offering unto the Lord. Seven days shalt thou prepare every day a goat for a sin offering: they shall also prepare a young bullock, and a ram out of the flock without blemish. Seven days shall they purge the altar and purify it; and they shall consecrate themselves. And when these days are expired, it shall be, that upon the eighth day, and soforward, the priests shall make your burnt offerings upon the altar, and your peace offerings; and I will accept you, saith the Lord God.

I would like to make several points about these verses. If Jesus died for the sins of mankind, as Christians have been taught, why does mankind have to make sin offerings in the New World Order? One should also note that in the New World Order, there is never any mention of the arts, music, theater, sporting events, or any leisure activity of any kind. Mankind becomes a slave who must cook for and care for the Annunaki on a daily basis. There is no mention that mankind retains any creative ability whatsoever. The genetic manipulation of mankind is working; man is slowly being turned into a biological robot. Mankind is forced to perform very tedious, monotonous tasks in order to continue the dumbing-down process.

The Annunaki initially created mankind to be a race of slaves. They created us through a process of genetic engineering. They created mankind by taking an egg from a hominid they called ape-woman. They mixed the DNA from ape-woman with clay, bitumens, and the blood of an Annunaki male. The Adam was produced. The Annunaki have continued to be involved with a huge experiment in genetic engineering ever since. Mankind serves as the guinea pigs for this experiment. The goal of this experiment is to produce a perfect slave. The ultimate fate of mankind depends upon the outcome of this experiment. If successful, the Annunaki will produce a slave that has no feelings, no emotions, and very limited mental ability. This slave will be given the food of life and water of life; they will have to exist in this condition for thousands of years. We must definitely alter the outcome of this experiment, or else the fate of mankind will be a very dismal one.

It is also quite likely that Earth will undergo a great natural disaster when Nibiru comes near Earth during its next orbit of the sun. This disaster will most likely be caused by a huge asteroid or perhaps a number of asteroids striking the Earth. The asteroids will have been dislodged from the asteroid belt by the passage of Nibiru. Mankind will be almost totally eliminated from the face of the Earth from this huge disaster. This should occur around AD 3400.

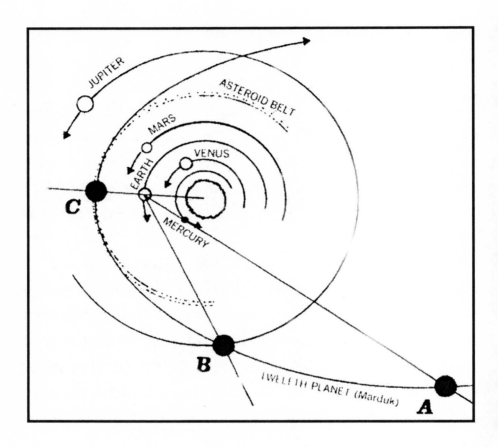

The Next Return of Nibiru

The schematic chart shown above illustrates the three crucial points where Nibiru can be observed and charted from Earth. Point A is when Nibiru aligns with Mercury and is the first opportunity to see Nibiru in Earth's skies. As it comes closer to Earth, it will appear to rise in the Earth's skies and will cross the orbit of Jupiter at point B. Point C is the place where Nibiru struck Tiamat, forming Earth, the moon, and asteroid belt. However, as Nibiru travels from point B to point C during its next return, asteroids will be displaced. They will shower Earth and cause a huge natural disaster that will kill most of the human race around AD 3400.

The fate of mankind was scripted by the Annunaki. In the occult, it is a common practice to inform the victim of their impending murder or sacrifice well in advance of its occurrence. The Annunaki have done just that in regard to mankind. This pronouncement of the fate of mankind is found in the Bible. One such pronouncement can be found in Isaiah 24:6–11:

> Therefore hath the curse devoured the earth, and they that dwell therein are desolate: therefore the inhabitants of the earth are burned, and few men left. The new wine mourneth, the vine languisheth, all the merryhearted do sigh. The mirth of tabrets ceaseth, the noise of them that rejoice endeth, the joy of the harp ceaseth. They

shall not drink wine with a song; strong drink
shall be bitter to them that drink it. The city of
confusion is broken down: every house is shut
up, that no man may come in. There is a crying
for wine in the streets; all joy is darkened, the
mirth of the land is gone.

The verses above describe the decimation of mankind
that occurs when Nibiru returns around AD 3400.
As I have stated before, the Bible is a masterpiece of
revelation. However, one's fate is not one's destiny. One's
destiny cannot be altered. One's fate can be altered. We
must alter the fate of mankind that was decreed by the
Annunaki. That will be accomplished by the Grandest
Rebellion.

The Annunaki are far more advanced both
technologically and culturally than mankind is. They
are much more intelligent than we are. They now own
about 75 percent of the wealth of the entire world. They
control all the multinational corporations and most of
the media outlets. They control all governments and
the military operations of those governments. They
control all religions on this Earth. They have used the
pharmaceutical industry and the health care systems
around the world to make mankind less healthy than
we should otherwise be. They have altered our genetics
and our immune systems. They have put chemicals in

our food, in our water, and in our atmosphere that affect us in negative ways. They watch us, manipulate us, and control our minds in order to make us do their bidding. In light of all these factors, how can a rebellion possibly be successful?

Humans have a few things in our favor. We far outnumber the Annunaki. Two heads are better than one; five, ten, one hundred, or one thousand to one is increasingly even better. Mankind has the capacity to be kind, to be compassionate, and to love another human; we can also exhibit these traits toward another species. I have observed these traits being expressed many times during my sixty-nine plus years on this Earth. I am not convinced that the Annunaki possess such traits. Perhaps we inherited those traits from ape-woman. The Annunaki might need to alter their genetic experiment in such a way that they acquire some ape-woman genes.

The Annunaki have also made a huge mistake. It seems that all criminals do make a mistake that eventually leads to their downfall. The mistake that the Annunaki made is that they acquired much of their wealth and much of their power over mankind from being dishonest and deceptive. In the long run, those tactics are never successful. Mankind can win the rebellion; the fate of mankind that has been scripted by the Annunaki can be altered. In order to do so, mankind must devise a plan, commit to the plan, and be totally dedicated to carry out the plan.

Most great achievements begin with one person having an idea. Oftentimes, the idea arises out of necessity. Others are recruited who believe in the idea. Even a small group of people can successfully achieve the fulfillment of the goal. The American Revolution is an example of such an occurrence. Perhaps the greatest example of this process is the creation of mankind itself.

Enki had an idea to create a slave race of beings to mine the gold for the Annunaki. The Annunaki had mutinied and refused to continue the gold-mining process. The work was backbreaking. A need arose that caused Enki to have his idea. He discussed the idea with his half sister, Ninharsag. She was the chief medical officer for the Annunaki. They, in turn, recruited a small group to help them. The Adam was produced. Mankind has become what we are today as a result of the idea of Enki.

The fate of mankind is in great jeopardy. We have a need. I have an idea about how this need can be met. I would like to discuss my idea with a few people in order to see whether there are others who see the same need that I do. If there are others who believe as I do, we need to put our heads together and devise a plan. In the remainder of this book, I will outline some general steps that I believe must be taken in order for the plan to become a reality. If man is going to be able to alter the fate that was scripted for him by the Annunaki, the process needs to begin soon. The New World Order will be put in place around AD 2160. We only have about 150 years to accomplish a lot of things if we are going to alter the fate of mankind. I hope that some of you will join me in this effort. We can defeat the Annunaki, but it will require a great deal of effort by many people.

Chapter 2

THE GROUP

I have not discussed my idea with a single person yet. The book publishers tell me that it will take another sixty to ninety days before this book reaches the market. After reading the book, I hope that some will contact me to discuss my idea. If that should happen, we will determine whether a core group can be formed to go forward with the Grandest Rebellion.

The first thing that this group must do is to agree that we will be totally open and honest with each other regardless of the consequences. We must agree that we will be completely open and transparent in regard to our plan. We will tell the rest of mankind as well as the Annunaki exactly what we plan to do. The Annunaki have told us what they plan to do in the Bible. We must counter that by doing likewise.

Our attitude must be that we have a common belief, that we recognize a need, and that this is what we are going to do to take care of that need, so stop us if you can. We must be totally honest with each other as well as with the rest of the world. In order for the Grandest Rebellion to be successful, absolute honesty is a necessity. I cannot stress enough how important it is that each and every person who is involved must absolutely and completely commit to being honest in all their endeavors.

Another step that the group must take is that they must study the Bible and become completely convinced about what it says. No one can just accept my interpretation for what the Bible says. Each member of the group must spend enough time with the Bible that they have absolutely no doubt about the proper interpretation of it. Only the truth can set one free from the Annunaki being able to control one's mind. The truth will set you free, but the Annunaki will kill you if you become a problem for them. The Annunaki have no regard for human life. To them, we are just a laboratory animal that has become too noisy and boisterous. One will not be able to totally commit to the rebellion unless they are fully convinced about the message given to mankind by the Annunaki. The message is disguised, but it rings out loudly and clearly when the Bible is understood.

Once the core group is formed, each member of the group must be totally dedicated to meeting on a regular basis in order to devise the specifics of the plan. The meetings may be held in private initially. As the group expands, the meetings will probably be held over the Internet. The meetings will be completely open and transparent. Any person from any nation and any persuasion will be invited to participate. We must take advantage of the fact that we far outnumber the Annunaki. We will need the thoughts, ideas, and input from as many people as possible.

The group will need to attract members from all walks of life to participate in the rebellion. We need to attract members from commerce and industry, from the media, from banking, from the sciences, from the arts, from government, from the military, from religion, and even from the Annunaki if possible. Enki might be a candidate. We need to attract geneticists, astronomers, theologians, physicians, engineers, and financiers to name only a few. The rebellion will be a massive project, but it can be done.

The entire group must agree not to resort to any form of aggression or violence. This must be a peaceful rebellion. Eventually, mankind must refuse to participate in the war at Armageddon (it occurs around AD 2160). If mankind decided today to never participate in another war, tremendous damage would be done to the Annunaki agenda. Mankind will be taunted and coerced into participating in the war at Armageddon in horrific ways during the Great Tribulation. To participate in that war will only serve to give Jesus the revenge on mankind that he has been programmed to seek. It will also give him an excuse for killing millions of humans. If mankind refuses to participate in that war, the New World Order will not occur exactly as scripted. It might never happen at all. The horrific conditions that are to be imposed upon mankind at that time will also be altered or will never occur.

The Annunaki may succeed in killing me: if so, another who is wiser than me will take my place. They may succeed in killing you; if so, another who is wiser than you will take your place. Violence and aggression will not benefit mankind in any way. As difficult as it will be, the group must adhere to the highest moral and ethical standards. Once the core group is formed and other participants are attracted, the specifics of the plan can be formulated. Priorities for carrying out the plan will include some things that will be discussed in subsequent chapters of this book.

Chapter 3

THE FEDERAL RESERVE BANK

I believe that one of the top priorities of the Grandest Rebellion must be to get rid of the Federal Reserve Bank (the Fed). That will be a huge undertaking in itself, but it has been done before. Once accomplished, the USA must encourage all nations to do likewise. Since this is such an important step, I am going to take a little time to explain some things about this dishonest monetary system. But before doing so, I will tell you what some others have had to say about it.

Louis McFadden, a Republican senator from Pennsylvania once said,

> We have in this country one of the most corrupt institutions the world has ever known.

I refer to the Federal Reserve Board. This evil institution has impoverished the people of the United States—and has practically bankrupted our government. It has done this through the corrupt practices of the moneyed vultures who control it.

Thomas Jefferson said,

If the American people ever allow private banks to control the issue of their currency, first by inflation, then by deflation, the banks and the corporations which grow around them will deprive the people of all property until their children wake up homeless on the continent their fathers conquered.

The late Dr. Carroll Quigley said,

The powers of financial capitalism had another far-reaching aim, nothing less than to create a world system of financial control in private hands able to dominate the political system of each country and the economy of the world as a whole. This system was to be controlled in a feudalist fashion by the central banks of the world acting in concert, by secret agreements arrived at in frequent private meetings and conferences. Each central bank sought to manipulate foreign exchanges, to influence the level of economic activity in the country, and to influence cooperative politicians by subsequent economic rewards in the business world.

Representative Charles A. Lindbergh, a Republican from Minnesota and the father of the famous aviator, said,

> The financial system has been turned over to the Federal Reserve Board. That board administers the finance system by authority of a purely profiteering group. The system is private, conducted for the sole purpose of obtaining the greatest possible profits from the use of other people's money.

Senator Barry Goldwater, a Republican from Arizona said,

> Most Americans have no real understanding of the operation of the international moneylenders. The accounts of the Federal Reserve System have never been audited. It operates outside the control of congress and manipulates the credit of the United States.

Dr. Ron Paul is a Republican member of the House of Representatives. Just this year he has become chairman of the house subcommittee that is supposed to oversee the actions of the Federal Reserve Bank. This subcommittee has never done anything to oversee the actions of the Federal Reserve Bank. However, Dr. Paul is a true patriot who understands how sinister our monetary system is. He is also brutally honest. The Annunaki have not been able to bribe him or buy his vote during the entire time that he has been in congress (since the late seventies). Dr. Paul has introduced a bill to audit the Fed. Everyone who reads this book should contact Dr. Paul, their congressman, and both senators from their state. The politicians should be encouraged to audit the Fed, then to eliminate them from this nation.

Thomas Jefferson said,

> I sincerely believe that banking institutions are more dangerous to our liberties than standing armies. The issuing power should be taken from the banks and restored to the people to whom it properly belongs.

James Madison said,

> History records that the money changers have used every form of abuse, intrigue, deceit and

violent means possible to maintain their control over governments by controlling money and its issuance.

Woodrow Wilson said,

Some of the biggest men in the United States, in the field of commerce and manufacture, are afraid of somebody, are afraid of something. They know there is a power somewhere so organized, so subtle, so watchful, so interlocked, so complete, so pervasive that they had better not speak above their breath when they speak in condemnation of it.

Abraham Lincoln said,

The money power preys upon the nation in times of peace and conspires against it in times of adversity. It is more despotic than monarchy, more insolent than aristocracy, more selfish than bureaucracy.

There is ample evidence now to indicate that Lincoln was assassinated because he wanted to get rid of the Fed. There is also evidence that John Kennedy and his brother were assassinated for the same reason.

Our founding fathers recognized the inherent evil in our banking system. Many, if not all, of our subsequent presidents have as well. Our congressman and senators, throughout the history of this nation, have also known that the Fed is extremely harmful to the prosperity of this nation. I ask the reader of this book, why have we not been able to eliminate the Fed?

We were strong enough to gain our independence from the strongest nation on Earth at that time, Great Britain. Yet even though we have always recognized the danger of the central banks, we have not been able to eliminate them. Is it reasonable to assume that the Annunaki were very instrumental in helping the colonies free themselves from Great Britain?

We know that George Washington was a member of a secret society, the Freemasons. There is a commemorative plaque in Washington DC that says,

George Washington

Freemason

And

First President of the United States of America

I find it very strange that a commemorative plaque in Washington DC places more importance on the fact that George Washington was a Freemason than on the fact that he was our first president. There is also a famous picture of him wearing his Masonic apron and other Masonic regalia. Washington DC was designed and laid out by the Freemasons. There are many Masonic symbols involved in the design of Washington DC.

Is it possible that the land that became the United States of America was known to have so many natural resources that the Annunaki wanted a bank here? And are two banks, one in Great Britain and one here, not better than one in Great Britain with branches here? If the Annunaki got kicked out of the banking business in one or the other nation (which has occurred), they would still be making lots of money with the other bank. Is it not perfectly clear that the Annunaki run our banks, control our government, and will someday destroy us? Is it not also evident that they will perform any sort of heinous act that is required in order to maintain their control?

The Fed can print as much money as they want whenever they want. If they print a lot of money and put it into the marketplace, it causes each dollar that you have to be worth less. That is inflation. As a result of this increase in money, prices rise. Money becomes relatively easy to borrow from the banks. Interest rates also rise.

The banks make a lot of money charging high interest. At the same time, they also sell a lot of their assets at inflated prices. They make more money.

When the Fed decides to decrease the money supply by taking money out of the marketplace, prices decrease. Money becomes difficult to borrow. Interest rates are low; the banks save a lot of money because they pay a small interest to holders of CDs and other bank notes. The Fed then buys assets at greatly reduced prices. They make lots of money whether the nation is suffering from inflation or deflation. There are numerous other ways that they can make money from this very evil and very dishonest system as well.

One very dishonest way that they make money is called fractional reserve banking. Under this system, the central banks can loan you money that they do not even have. The bank may actually have one hundred thousand dollars on reserve. But they may loan much more than that to borrowers. They may loan ten times or more money than they actually possess. They collect interest on the number of dollars loaned even though they never had it to begin with. We have recently seen what can happen when they loan billions of dollars that they do not have, create such poverty that the borrowers cannot repay the loans, and thus have huge defaults on the loans. No big deal; their puppet (President Obama, in this case) just replaces the money lost by the banks with taxpayer dollars. The Annunaki get richer; the humans get poorer. Even a dumbed-down slave, such as me, could make lots of money if I were allowed to operate the way our central bank does.

The goal of the Annunaki has always been to acquire all the wealth on Earth from the first day they set foot on this planet searching for gold until today. They make a very interesting comment in Ecclesiastes 10:19:

> A feast is made for laughter, and wine maketh
> merry: but money answereth all things.

To the Annunaki, money is, indeed, the answer for everything. It will remain so until mankind wakes up and rebels.

The Annunaki decided to scatter the language of mankind because of the incident at the Tower of Babel. Mankind should scatter the power of the central banks. The issuance of money should be returned to the people. Each state should be allowed to issue money. The large cities should also be allowed to issue money. The monopoly on money must be removed or the fate of mankind may be unalterable. If mankind does not put a stop to this private banking network, we will all wake up homeless on the planet upon which we were created.

Chapter 4

GOVERNMENTS, DICTATORS, AND
POWERS OF AUTHORITY

I do not care whether a nation is governed by a republic, like the United States is supposed to be, or by some other form of government. The ruling authority may be a dictator, a democracy, or any other form of governmental body the people of that nation choose to have. The form of government that any group of people choose to have is not nearly as important today as what the people who live in that country believe. The rebellion that must occur is not one of nation against nation; it is also not one of the citizenry of a nation against the government (or ruling authority) of that nation. The rebellion is one of mankind against the Annunaki. In this chapter of my book, I am going to discuss what the citizens of the

United States of America must do with our government in order to defeat the Annunaki. The citizenry of each nation will, hopefully, gain insight from this discussion. The citizenry of each nation may then decide what the best course of action is for their nation. I am not saying that people from all nations should not join together to defeat the Annunaki; they should. I am saying that each nation should determine their form of government and their fate during and after the rebellion.

It should be obvious to most Americans that the powers who run our nation are not the officials who we elect to office. One should question whether that process is even worthwhile. It is extremely expensive and serves no useful purpose. I hope that after reading *The Grandest Deception*, you realize that the Bible is a story about the Annunaki (not about God); even if you do not, I do not understand how you could be awake in our world today and believe that our elected officials run our nation. They absolutely do not. One of the priorities of *The Grandest Rebellion* should be to correct that. The people who we elect to office must be answerable to the people who elect them; and in turn, they must accept their responsibility and run the nation in accordance with the wishes of the people. How can that be accomplished?

If one gives even the slightest thought to the electoral process that we have been deceived into developing, surely one would agree with me that it is total insanity.

The dumbing-down process has worked amazingly well in regard to the process we go through to elect our leaders. The general public and the businesses they own are deceived into donating many millions of dollars to the candidates. The candidates spend the large majority of this money on media advertising. The candidates then put on a real dog and pony show in the media; this consists of advertisements and debates that are always adversarial in nature. There is no accountability for the truth of any of this. The candidates have no concern whatsoever that they will ever be held accountable for their statements. So what value is all this to the public? There is none whatsoever. Well, the dog and pony show may provide some entertainment value; although it is nonsensical, it is quite comical at times.

The corporations who own the media outlets are owned and controlled by the Annunaki and their descendents. They make millions upon millions of dollars from the electoral process they have so cleverly designed and duped the people into participating in. The same lies, deceit, and advancement of the Annunaki agenda continue; we then fall for the same nonsense again in two, four, or six years on an even larger scale. Please do not donate any money to this process. In fact, the best policy is to simply ignore and not participate in the political process in any way until a plan can be devised to alter it.

I believe that our entire electoral process should be completely revised. The Annunaki use the media outlets as well as the Internet to their advantage. Mankind should do likewise. All federal elections could be held through use of the Internet and media outlets. In this way, we would save billions of dollars. Let us use the presidential election as an example.

Any person who wanted to run for president could set up a web page; Facebook, Twitter, etc., could be used. Each candidate could spend an allotted amount of time explaining to the American people what his or her policies would be. Each citizen could maintain a visual record of what the candidate said he/she would do if elected. There would be no need for a party system. Each candidate would be responsible for paying their own expenses. The expenses incurred would be minimal so that practically anyone could afford to run for president. A primary election could be held. The top five or ten vote getters could then be given free airtime on TV to reiterate their plan and their promises. A final election could be held. Any president who did not make every effort to implement his/her plan and keep his/her promises should quickly be impeached and removed from office.

An impeachment process could also be devised, which could occur via the Internet. The American people could impeach the president. American people would not have to endure the nonsense we went through with the impeachment process of Bill Clinton.

All elected federal positions could be carried out in a similar fashion. By employing the use of the Internet to elect our federal officials, the American people would be much more informed about what is going on in the world of politics. Tremendous amounts of money would be saved; this money could be placed back into our economy to be used for some useful purpose. There would be much less likelihood that our elected officials could be bribed or would accept a bribe. The American people could see to it that those who were elected kept their promises and did what they pledged to do; if they did not, they could quickly be removed from office. Government of the people, by the people, and for the people would be a reality.

The American people would receive many other benefits from such a process as well. Those benefits are too numerous to mention in this book; let me just say that our entire federal government could probably be run over the Internet from the comfort of the homes of our elected officials. Washington DC could be turned into a national museum and become a tourist attraction, or it could be used for some other useful purpose. Practically any use of it would be better than its present one.

If a small group of people (the Group) who understand the problem can be formed, if they will choose to be perfectly honest in all their endeavors, if they will agree to remain totally nonviolent in all their activities, and if they will commit to seeing the rebellion through to its conclusion, they will be successful.

If the human race chose to be honest and nonviolent, nations would only need to pass two laws. No person would be allowed to harm another person in any way. Law number two would be that all humans have to be honest. If either of these laws were violated, the penalty for such would simply be to remove the violator from society. It is really quite simple. We would live in a utopian world. The entire world would become a Garden of Eden.

What is required of one in order to be honest and nonviolent? One must make a decision to live their life in such a manner. One would have to keep that decision in the back of their mind at all times. One would have to commit to adhering to that decision. Adhering to that decision might be difficult for some at first. But with time, living in that manner would become second nature to that individual. If our children were taught from birth to live their lives in such a manner, if they observed others living that way as they grew up, and if they knew that there would be the severest penalty if they did not adhere to those two laws, they would obey.

Is mankind capable of making such a decision and committing to the adherence of such a decision? Most humans are quite capable of doing those two things, especially if they are encouraged by others to do so.

Some, unfortunately, are not capable. The ones who are not capable would have to be removed from society.

If mankind creates such a society someday, wonderful things would occur over a period of time. In such a society, the process of evolution would be allowed to occur without interruption or alteration. Evolution is actually God's way of improving all living organisms. The processes of natural selection and survival of the fittest allow the positive traits and characteristics of living organisms to be passed from generation to generation. Each generation receives more positive traits than the last. The negative traits are slowly eliminated. God's process of evolution ensures that human beings become wiser, healthier, and live longer lives over a period of time. I think that most people would agree that we are not seeing that happen in our world today. The reason that it is not occurring in our world today is that the Annunaki are intentionally altering the process. The perfect slave cannot be produced through the process of evolution. The discord that has been created between creationists and evolutionists is simply another example of how the Annunaki have deceived us. It is definitely time for mankind to stop engaging in such childish and foolish quarrels. We have identified our enemy; we must now unite and defeat that enemy.

Some from the Group must agree to become involved in the business of politics. They must run for public office. The Group must have expanded to the point that they can elect their candidates to office. Those elected must accept their responsibility to run the government in accordance with the wishes of the public. They must rid the land of the Federal Reserve banking system and perform other duties that the public demands. They must begin to compete with the Annunaki. They should also work very hard to revolutionize our entire system of government.

I believe that the United States of America should begin to consider whether our form of government is good for mankind. We have indeed created a federal monster. We have far too many nonsensical laws. We have become so dishonest and corrupt that we ignore our Constitution. We even expect our citizenry to be dishonest and break these laws. If we had a limited number of laws, and if they were reasonable, we should expect that people obey them. We have actually developed a system that encourages people to be dishonest and to disobey our laws. We have developed a system that encourages our leaders to become dishonest, to accept bribes, and to ignore the well-being of our nation and our people. We have developed a system that encourages our people to have a poor work ethic, to not accept the responsibility for their own well-being, and to believe that the government should steal from one in order to give to another. Such a system cannot endure because it breeds discontent among the people, and because it is dishonest (exactly what the Annunaki want).

If one examines the form of government that the Annunaki have deceived us into developing in the United States with an open mind, I believe that most will soon realize how harmful it is to our nation. The entire political system in the USA is cleverly designed to breed discord among the participants in the system and among the people in our country.

We are told that the three branches of our federal government are supposed to provide "checks and balances" between the three branches. I do not believe that that is what actually occurs. It appears that rather than checks and balances, what actually occurs is a struggle for power between the three branches. Each branch seeks to impose its will on the other two branches; the results are discord between the branches and discord among the people (exactly what the Annunaki want). If one examines the three branches of our government on an individual basis, there are major flaws in the design of each.

The judicial branch is designed to be adversarial in nature; our entire justice system is adversarial by its very design. There may be some, but I do not recall ever seeing a Supreme Court decision of an important matter that was unanimous. The Supreme Court judges appear to disagree about every topic. Why does the system place people in office for life who are not going to agree on anything? I believe that that is exactly why it was designed in the manner it was, i.e., to ensure that discord would be perpetuated. I do not believe that lifetime appointments are ever a good thing. Situations and circumstances change; justices should be changed as well.

The legislative branch, of course, is even more adversarial. More people are involved in this branch, and more disagreement is guaranteed because of the adversarial design of its structure. Having a two-party system ensures that the members of the two parties will disagree on many topics. It also ensures that the two parties will develop different goals, different priorities, and different planks at their conventions; this ensures discord (just what the Annunaki want).

The executive branch is the easiest for the Annunaki. They only have to control one person. They support candidates from both parties; the Annunaki do not care which party wins. Should a candidate win who has not been supported by the Annunaki, he will be tolerated as long as he does not create too many problems. Should one like Abraham Lincoln, John Kennedy, or Ronald Reagan win (none of them were related to or controlled by the Annunaki), the Annunaki will simply assassinate them (or try to in Reagan's case). Even though the attempted assassination was not successful in the case of President Reagan, the Annunaki were able to see to it that the Great Communicator was unable to effectively communicate in his latter years. He was stricken with Alzheimer's disease.

Alzheimer's disease is an artificially produced malady. There is no mention of this horribly incapacitating ailment in any of the old medical literature or in any of the ancient writings. Alzheimer's disease is a product of the genetic engineering experiment being carried out by the Annunaki in their attempt to produce the perfect slave. For those of you who have a family member or close friend who has suffered from or is currently suffering from this horribly debilitating illness, you have the Annunaki to thank for it.

The Annunaki agenda continues, mankind continues to be dumbed down, unremitting physical hardships for most continue, spiritual decay of an alarming magnitude continues, and the process repeats itself in four years on a larger and grander scale. We are just not very smart compared to the Annunaki. It is time to make radical changes in our government and in our political processes.

The Annunaki plan to make radical changes in all political processes in the entire world. They have decided to create a New World Order. A one-world government is planned. Jesus will be the dictator of this worldwide, central government. This government will wreak havoc upon mankind, will steal all things of value, and will greatly increase the dumbing-down process. Mankind should make every effort to ensure that these things do not occur.

I believe that the new government order created in the USA should be exactly the opposite of what the Annunaki propose for their new world government. Power and authority should be decentralized as much as possible. The only federal laws in the USA should be the two I mentioned earlier. Each individual should be held accountable for upholding these two laws and living by them. If an individual breaks one of these laws, the family of that individual should see to it that the violator is removed from society. Should the family not be able to perform their duty, the people in the nearest village, town, or city should assist them. Should the entire family become violators, the nearest village, town, or city should remove the family. If entire villages, towns, or cities become violators, the people of the state should remove them. Should an entire state become violators, the people of the USA should remove the people of that state from society.

Each family, each township, and each state should then develop any additional laws, rules, or regulations that they deem necessary to govern their respective domains as long as these laws do not violate the two federal laws in any way. Each individual should be free to develop a personal relationship with the god of their understanding without trying to impose their beliefs on any other person. Each person should be free to live their life as they desire as long as they do not violate either federal law. I believe that the best system and the best living conditions for mankind would occur from this approach.

No institution or entity should place taxes on anyone. All federal, state, or city taxes should be completely voluntary as they once were in this nation. Any money loaned should be done so without charging interest. Interest is nothing more than a dishonest tax. It also breeds discord between the parties involved in the transaction. Each state should be allowed to issue money; the large cities should be allowed to issue money if they choose to do so. If an individual became wealthy enough, the individual could also be allowed to issue money. No fractional reserve banking could occur because that is dishonest.

Chapter 5

EVIL BEYOND BELIEF

The evil that the Annunaki have perpetrated upon mankind is almost beyond the ability of the human mind to comprehend. It is quite possible that one of our great wars was caused because of the genetic experiment. This is also the saddest war that the USA ever participated in because it pitted brother against brother at times; it is called the Civil War.

The Annunaki had moved their gold mining operation to Africa soon after landing on Earth. We have found mining shafts in Africa that are over two hundred thousand years old. Mankind, the Adam, was created in Africa. The genetic engineering experiment was conceived and begun in Africa. It just so happened that the blacks of Africa were among the first to be genetically manipulated.

The circumstances were manipulated in such a way that some of these blacks were captured and brought to the USA. Some suffered horrible atrocities so that the Annunaki could test whether they had produced the perfect slave. All the slaves brought to America suffered great indignation. The whole nasty affair was contrived so that the Annunaki could evaluate the progress of their genetic experiment.

The positive part of the whole mess is that the black race proved to be extremely resilient. We should all commend them for their tenacity and inner strength. They did not give in to the Annunaki and did not become meek, mild, perfect slaves. I hope that we still have the same resolve today.

The Annunaki have killed billions of people in the wars that they have masterminded. They have killed millions with the backbreaking, arduous types of labor that they have imposed. They have killed millions or perhaps even billions more as a result of the genetic engineering experiment they are conducting. As horrible as these deaths are, the deaths may not be the worst evil committed.

Far more heinous than the deaths may be the torture, pain, and suffering imposed upon mankind by the Annunaki. We know that things such as burning people alive while they were tied to a stake, sawing them in half, skinning them alive, and many other unspeakable forms of torture have been imposed upon mankind. The Annunaki have created unbelievably cruel human beings through their genetic experiment who have done extremely cruel things to other humans.

The cruelty that has resulted from the deception of mankind by the Annunaki is, indeed, hard to fathom. For instance, the caste system that has been created in India is atrocious. In India, about 85 percent of the nine hundred million or so people who live there practice the Hindu religion. To the Hindu, almost all life is sacred, yet millions of their people live in abject poverty and starve to death. The Aryans invaded India around the time of Moses. The Aryans became the rulers and the elite. They devised the caste system and the complex religion of Hinduism. Hinduism is simply another branch of the Brotherhood of the Serpent. The caste system set up by the Aryans dictates that every person is born into the caste of his father; one may never leave that caste. The top level of the caste system belongs to the Aryans; they continue to rule India. The bottom level of the caste system is occupied by those considered to be "outcasts" or "untouchables"; these live in abject poverty, suffer greatly, and can never change their caste.

Around 525 BCE, an Indian prince by the name of Siddhartha Gautama opposed the caste system. He eventually became known as Buddha. Buddhism spread rapidly; Buddha was not worshipped as a god. He was respected as a great thinker. He devised a religion by which an individual might achieve spiritual freedom through one's efforts. Buddha may have been on the right track; however, his teachings were perverted over time by the Annunaki. Buddha knew that he had not created a method by which mankind could achieve spiritual freedom; he did promise that a Mettaya (friend) would come someday who would have the knowledge to complete the task. The Brotherhood has caused Buddhism as well as the legend of Mettaya to decay into the rot that it is today.

The cruelest joke that has been played on the Muslims must certainly be the deception that has caused them to believe that they should kill all infidels who refuse to convert to Islam. Mohammed was born around AD 570; he died in AD 632. His teachings have resulted in a series of bloody wars that have caused untold numbers of humans to be killed. Organizations arising from the Brotherhood supported both sides of the bloody wars between Muslims and Christians during the wars known as the Crusades.

The Muslims are descendents of Ishmael, the firstborn son of Abraham. The bloody wars continue today between the descendents of Ishmael and the descendents of Isaac, Abraham's second son. Many young Muslim men have also been killed because of their belief that they would immediately be transported to paradise where a harem of beautiful women awaited them if they were killed while attempting to kill the infidels. Cruel! Cruel! Cruel!

Perhaps the cruelest thing that was done to the Israelites was that they were told by the Annunaki that they were God's chosen people. This teaching has caused many Jewish deaths; it has also caused the Jewish people to suffer great atrocities such as the Holocaust. Eventually, it will cause all nations to join together in order to attempt to defeat the nation of Israel at the battle of Armageddon. Many humans will be killed, and horrible atrocities will be committed by both sides of this conflict, according to the Annunaki.

Enlil has provided advanced technology to the nation of Israel. Israel has the most powerful military force in the world today. Israel already has the military capability to defeat the combined military might of the rest of the world. The USA continues to give Israel huge sums of money in foreign aid, which they will use to strengthen their military even more. Israel will slaughter all people in the world, including Americans, when the time is right. Many of our very deceived and dumbed-down theologians rant on about how we should support Israel because they are God's chosen people. That is about the dumbest thing that we can do. After Israel slaughters us, the Annunaki will slaughter any remaining Israelis who do not make very good slaves. If the Grandest Rebellion is successful, this carnage can be avoided.

And finally, in my mind, there is no doubt that the cruelest thing done to those of the Christian faith is the deception about Jesus, which includes the deception about the route to spiritual freedom (salvation). The message of Jesus is contained throughout the New Testament. Perhaps the most damaging aspects of this message are found in the letters of Paul, the primary author of the New Testament.

I believe that one of the most damaging verses found in the entire Bible relating to Christians is Romans 10:9:

> That if thou shalt confess with thy mouth the Lord Jesus, and shalt believe in thine heart that God hath raised him from the dead, thou shalt be saved.

This verse has been taken to mean that one can attain spiritual freedom (salvation) by simply stating that Jesus is Lord and savior and believing that that deception is true. This belief has been twisted further by some Christians to mean that nothing can alter the result once the statement is made, i.e., once saved, always saved. Very young children make the statement, believe it, and the process is supposed to be complete. Those who believes the doctrine of "once saved, always saved" believes that it is safe and secure for all eternity because they made one statement or gave one testimony.

For most of my life, I thought I was what is called a born-again Christian. I sincerely believed the things about Jesus and salvation that I was taught as a child. When I had my only begotten son, I named him Paul; he was named after the apostle to the gentiles. As dumbed down as I was, I never was bad enough to fall for "once saved, always saved." It would be very nice if that nonsense were true; unfortunately, that belief is far from being true. What does belief in that doctrine actually do?

Belief in the doctrine, "once saved, always saved" actually accomplishes exactly what the Annunaki intended it to accomplish. It essentially halts any further spiritual development in the individual. Human nature, being what it is, almost guarantees that the person with a belief such as that one will do one of two things. One will stop studying and seeking the truth because one feels that the goal has already been attained, or any further study by that individual will be twisted and skewed in an attempt to make the information fit the belief. Their study becomes invalid because it is biased and dishonest. As a consequence of this belief, the Christian has reached a standstill in his spiritual development; he makes no more progress until belief in that false doctrine is removed. That is extremely cruel.

If the doctrine that one could attain spiritual freedom by making a statement were true, people who make the statement should immediately be able to leave their body, travel around with God, and enjoy his universe. I have yet to see a single one of the "saved" do that. I have seen people who have made the statement and believed in their heart, however, later become alcoholics, drug addicts, pedophiles, and rapists. I am sure that many have become even more heinous. The truth should be obvious to anyone who has not been dumbed down too much.

Chapter 6

RELIGION, SECRET SOCIETIES, AND SPIRITUALITY

Is religion a godly thing? It is not. Every religion on this planet is either Annunaki-made or man-made. It is therefore flawed. James 1:27, says,

> Pure religion and undefiled before God and the
> Father is this, To visit the fatherless and widows
> in their affliction, and to keep himself unspotted
> from the world.

Every religion on Earth breeds discord between humans. The Koran even says that the Muslims are to kill all infidels if they do not agree to convert to the religion of Islam. Mankind should eliminate religion from their lives. Each individual should be allowed to develop relationships between themselves and others, as well as between themselves and God, without the hindrance of religion interfering with the development of those relationships.

Some may say that I am proposing rather radical changes. Mankind has not become any better at loving and caring for our fellow man than we were when Cain killed Abel; I think that radical changes are needed. The Israelites and Canaanites have been killing each other for about four thousand years for no good reason; I think that radical changes are needed. The history of mankind since the flood has been a history of warfare for about thirteen thousand years now; I think that radical changes are needed.

There are several very good examples in the Bible that refer to how the Annunaki have deceived, conned, and manipulated mankind into fighting nonsensical wars. One such example can be found in Joshua 11:19–20:

> There was not a city that made peace with the children of Israel, save the Hivites the inhabitants of Gibeon: all other they took in battle. For it was of the Lord to harden their hearts, that they should come against Israel in battle, that he might destroy them utterly, and that they might have no favour, but that he might destroy them, as the Lord commanded Moses.

These verses say that one city surrendered peacefully when they saw the might of the Israeli army. They also say that God caused the other cities to fight just so he could completely kill all the inhabitants of that city. This is typical Annunaki strategy. If you believe that God acts in this way, you are one sick puppy. I will not bother to describe the others, but there are many other places in the Bible that say God "hardened" some heart in order to demonstrate his power or cause some terrible thing to occur. I assure you that it was not God but the Annunaki who did these things.

The Annunaki had been deceiving mankind for many years prior to the flood. Noah had been on the submarine for over a year. When he was able to debark, the first thing he had to do was build an altar and make sacrifices to the Annunaki. The deception of mankind continued.

When the Israelites were allowed to go into the promised land, they were told that their marriages must only occur between members of their own clan. They did not follow these instructions in Ezra 10:10–11:

> And Ezra the priest stood up, and said unto them, Ye have transgressed, and have taken strange wives, to increase the trespass of Israel. Now therefore make confession unto the Lord God of your fathers, and do his pleasure: and separate yourselves from the people of the land, and from the strange wives.

The instructions about marriage were given in order to expedite the genetic experiment that was taking place. Record keeping, documentation of outcomes, and so forth was simply made much easier if the marriages of the Israelites were controlled. The experiment could be moved along at a more rapid pace as well. The deception of mankind continued.

A rather cruel spiritual joke was played on the pharaohs of Egypt. They were told that they could avoid the fate of humans and join the gods in heaven if they followed the instructions of the Annunaki. They were instructed to have their bodies mummified. They were told that their preserved bodies would be brought back to life so that they could join the gods in heaven. The pharaohs were busy helping to make slaves out of their fellow humans; the Annunaki were busy making fools out of the pharaohs.

The cruelty displayed toward the pharaohs is mentioned in the Bible in Romans 9:16–18:

> So then it is not of him that willeth, nor of him that runneth, but of God that showeth mercy. For the scripture saith unto Pharoah, Even for this same purpose have I raised thee up, that I might show my power in thee, and that my name might be declared throughout all the earth.

This cruelty to the pharaohs was done in spite of the fact that the pharaohs were part Annunaki and part human, i.e., offspring of the sons of god cohabiting with the daughters of men. Or perhaps, it was done because they were part Annunaki and part human. At any rate, it is just another example of how the Annunaki control our minds, cause our spiritual decay, and continue to deceive us.

During the time of the pharaohs, spiritual knowledge was tremendously decreased. A secret society grew out of the Brotherhood of the Serpent, which became known as the "Mystery Schools." The Mystery Schools taught the pharaohs and priests spiritual knowledge, but true spiritual knowledge was twisted, altered, and restricted. Pharaohs, priests, and only a few others were allowed to attend these schools. They had to take a solemn oath not to write any of the information down or to reveal it to outsiders. The information had to be passed from generation to generation orally; most of the secret societies conduct their affairs in this way. The information could only be passed to other pharaohs, priests, and a few chosen ones. There is no quicker way to lose information than to pass it on orally and not write it down. The alterations of the information that surely occurred must have been quite amusing to the Annunaki. I am sure that they find some of our nonsensical, religious teachings amusing as well.

Moses of Bible fame must have surely attended the Mystery Schools. In Acts 7:20–22 we find the following:

> In which time Moses was born, and was exceeding fair, and nourished up in his father's house three months: And when he was cast out, Pharaoh's daughter took him up, and nourished him for her own son. And Moses was learned in all the wisdom of the Egyptians, and was mighty in words and in deeds.

Moses being "exceeding fair" reminds me of the birth of Noah, of underground evolution of the Annunaki, and of the sons of gods cohabiting with the daughters of men. Moses was quite likely part Annunaki. He was also tremendously deceived by the Mystery Schools. An Egyptian historian named Manetho had this to say about Moses around 300 BCE:

> Moses, a son of the tribe of Levi, educated in Egypt and initiated in Heliopolis, became a High Priest of the Brotherhood under the reign of Pharoah Amenhotep. He was elected by the Hebrews as their chief and he adapted to the ideas of his people the science and philosophy which he had obtained in the Egyptian mysteries; proofs of this are to be found in the symbol, in the Initiations,

and in the precepts and commandments—The dogma of an "only God" which he taught was the Egyptian Brotherhood interpretation and teaching of the Pharaoh who established the first monotheistic religion known to man.

This clearly says that Moses was trained and educated by the Brotherhood, Enlil's secret society. Is it any wonder that Moses did what the Annunaki wanted? Or is there any doubt that Moses was conned, manipulated, and deceived into doing so? I think not. The exodus, the wanderings through the desert and the instructions given to Moses did not come from God. Can you imagine God telling someone to go into a land and kill every man, woman, and child? How ridiculous!

The Bible says that Moses died when he was 120 years old and that he was buried by God. That could mean that he was taken to underground accommodations, given the food of life and the water of life, and that he is still wreaking havoc on mankind today. According to the Bible, he partnered with Jesus and Elijah to deceive three of the disciples of Jesus.

And after six days Jesus taketh Peter, James, and John his brother, and bringeth them up into an high mountain apart, And was transfigured before them; and his face did shine as the sun, and his raiment was white as the light. And behold, there appeared unto them Moses and Elias (Elijah) talking with him. Then answered Peter, and said unto Jesus, Lord, it is good for us to be here: if thou wilt, let us make here three tabernacles; one for thee, and one for Moses, and one for Elias. While he yet spake, behold, a bright cloud overshadowed them: and behold a voice out of the cloud, which said, This is my beloved Son, in whom I am well pleased; hear ye him. (Matthew 17:1–5)

This event occurred some 1,200 years after Moses was supposed to be dead and buried. Moses and Elijah may have been sent on this mission to help Jesus pull off the deception or to ensure that he did so. Jesus was still young and had not been completely tested by the Annunaki in regard to whether he would do all that they had told him to do.

There is a passage in the Revelation 11:3–2, that says,

And I will give power unto my two witnesses, and they shall prophesy a thousand two hundred and threescore days, clothed in sackcloth. These are the two olive trees, and the two candlesticks standing before the God of the earth. And if any man will hurt them, fire proceedeth out of their mouth, and devoureth their enemies: and if any man will hurt them, he must in this manner be killed. These have power to shut heaven, that it rain not in the days of their prophecy: and have power over waters to turn them to blood, and to smite the earth with all plagues, as often as they will. And when they shall have finished their testimony, the beast that ascendeth out of the bottomless pit shall make war against them, and shall overcome them, and kill them. And their dead bodies shall lie in the street of the great city, which spiritually is called Sodom and Egypt, where also our Lord was crucified. And they of the people and kindreds and tongues and nations shall see their dead bodies three days and an half, and shall not suffer their dead bodies to be put in graves. And they that dwell upon the earth shall rejoice over them, and make merry, and shall send gifts one to another, because these two prophets tormented them that dwell on the earth. And after three days and an half the Spirit of life from God entered into them, and they stood upon their feet; and great fear fell upon them which saw them. And they heard a great voice from heaven saying unto them, Come up hither. And they ascended up to heaven in a cloud; and their enemies beheld them.

These things occur just after Jesus returns and just before the battle at Armageddon. They occur during the Great Tribulation. I believe that the two witnesses are Moses and Jesus, both of whom have been terribly deceived and are quite angry at mankind. I stated earlier in this book that Enlil had succeeded in turning Jesus into an angry, vengeful monster; he has done the same to Moses. The people of Earth are also quite angry at Moses and Jesus and have now realized what the two of them have done. An interesting part of these verses to me is the mention of "kindreds." I believe that the kindreds are the part human, part Annunaki descendents who realize during the Great Tribulation that they have been deceived as well.

The part-human, part-Annunaki descendents (kindreds) who are alive today are members of the secret societies and comprise the Establishment. They are gladly doing the will of the Annunaki today. I would love to be able to have an honest discussion with the Bush, Clinton, or Rockefeller family (or any family who are Establishment) in order to find out what they really believe the truth to be. I feel quite sure that they have been deceived just as Moses, Jesus, and the kindreds were. Perhaps these families could learn the truth and be convinced to join the Grandest Rebellion. They would certainly be great allies if they are capable of being honest.

There was a famous Italian philosopher of the sixteenth-century AD who wrote several manuals about how to control mankind and deceive them so that humans would constantly be at odds with each other. These were how-to manuals about how to produce wars and how to control populations of humans. The philosopher's name was Niccolo Machiavelli. His how-to manuals have become literary classics. His conclusions were the following:

1. Initiate conflicts and "issues" that will cause people to fight among themselves rather than against the perpetrator.
2. Remain hidden from view as the true instigator of the conflicts.
3. Lend support to all warring parties.
4. Be viewed as the benevolent source which can solve the conflicts.

It would be difficult to state more plainly and succinctly what the Annunaki have done in this regard over the past four thousand years.

Since mankind has acquired such a paucity of spiritual knowledge, it is difficult to discuss the topic of spirituality. Initially, before the Brotherhood of the Serpent was corrupted by Enlil, the Brotherhood engaged in a pragmatic program of spiritual education. There was nothing mystical or ceremonial about their teachings. Their approach to the subject was strictly scientific. Spiritual knowledge could be learned and known just as any other branch of science could. The Brotherhood seemed to possess considerable data and information about spiritual matters. The spiritual data appeared to be quite accurate; however, a complete route to spiritual freedom had not been developed prior to Enlil corrupting the Brotherhood and taking control of it. Sadly, that information and data is now lost as far as mankind is concerned. Mankind possesses less knowledge concerning the route to spiritual freedom today than the Brotherhood had thousands of years ago.

I will readily admit that I possess very little spiritual knowledge. I do agree with the ancient teachings that spiritual knowledge can be learned and known just as any other branch of science can. Spiritual freedom and/or salvation, if you prefer, is not a matter of faith; that teaching is more of Enlil's distortion of the truth. I prefer the term of *spiritual freedom* over the term *salvation*; therefore, I will call spiritual freedom what most in this country would call salvation. Regardless of what we call it, all of us would like to attain it. I certainly am not going to try to tell anyone how to try to attain spiritual freedom; I do not know how to do that. I am also not trying to tell anyone what their perception of God should be; that is an individual thing.

Our best science states that our universe is expanding from the force of the big bang explosion. Physicists will surely disagree with the concept, but I think of the force from the big bang as being love. Thinking of the force as being love coming from God simply helps my simple little mind understand some other things about our world and our universe. I think of the force, love, as being what causes every atom, every particle, and everything to work the way it does in our universe. The Bible says that God is love.

When we throw a ball into the air, it goes away from us until the force of the throw is overcome by gravity, which causes the ball to return to Earth. I believe that when the force of the big bang is overcome, all that is in the universe will implode back upon itself, just as the ball returns to Earth. That process will continue until only a tiny speck of matter exists; another big bang will occur. God will express himself in another way with the next big bang. Many other big bangs may have occurred prior to this one; many others may occur after this one and continue to do so throughout eternity.

How do those who possess a soul fit into this picture? I think that each soul is eternal and is spirit. I perceive the soul as being a unit of awareness that knows that it exists; it is also aware that other units of awareness exist. I believe that when a soul enters a living body, it normally stays there until the body dies. However, I believe that the soul or spirit can leave the body; we have many examples of out-of-body experiences. I believe that when the goal of attaining spiritual freedom is finally realized, one is able to leave their body at will without causing the death of the body.

One then truly does have the best of both worlds. One can enjoy the world of the spirit and travel throughout the universe in that form; then, one can return to the body (or perhaps even another body) and enjoy the physical, emotional, and sensual pleasures associated with the body. What a deal.

A lot of study and hard work is required in order to attain spiritual freedom, but the reward for doing so is truly awesome. The Bible says in several places to "seek and ye shall find." Whatever amount of study and effort is required in order to attain spiritual freedom, the reward is more than worth the effort. Whatever sacrifice is required in order to ensure that mankind retains the ability to study and seek is also more than worth the effort. I sincerely hope that all of you are studying and seeking; I also hope that you will join me in the Grandest Rebellion in order to ensure that our descendents retain the ability to study and seek as well. I think that most would agree that to alter the fate of mankind that has been planned by the Annunaki is a noble cause.

Chapter 7

FAITH, PRAYER, AND WORKS

I stated earlier that attaining spiritual freedom is not a matter of faith, and it is not. At least, it is not in the sense that those of the Christian faith have been taught. Attaining spiritual freedom certainly has nothing to do with believing in Jesus; one can attain spiritual freedom without even believing in God. I believe that the process would be more difficult if there is no belief in a Supreme Being; however, I believe that it could be done. I also believe that immediately upon attaining spiritual freedom, one will realize that there is a Supreme Being. God does not need one's belief or one's faith in him. He is quite sufficient without it. Our beliefs and our faith have been misdirected by the Annunaki.

We all need to have faith, but that faith and belief should be in ourselves.

Each and every human should believe that they can attain spiritual freedom, and they should have enough faith in themselves to seek that attainment. Each person should realize that they are a part of God and his creation regardless of what they have done or not done in the past. Being part of God's creation makes each and every soul valuable. If one believes that they are valuable, that they have the ability to attain spiritual freedom, and that they are willing to work at it hard enough, I have no doubt that they will attain it someday. But Isaiah 55:6–7 says,

> Seek ye the Lord while he may be found, call
> ye upon him while he is near: Let the wicked
> forsake his way, and the unrighteous man his
> thoughts: and let him return unto the Lord, and
> he will have mercy upon him; and to our God,
> for he will abundantly pardon.

"While he may be found" implies that a time will come when God cannot be found or when spiritual freedom cannot be attained; most Christian theologians probably interpret that to mean that spiritual freedom cannot be attained after one dies. They are wrong. The soul or spirit is eternal; it can enter another body.

The inerrant word of God says that the spirit can enter another body; in fact, it even says that many souls can enter the same body.

> And he asked him, What is thy name? And he answered, saying, My name is Legion: for we are many. And he besought him much that he would not send them away out of the country. Now there was there nigh unto the mountains a great herd of swine feeding. And all the devils besought him, saying, Send us into the swine, that we may enter into them. And forthwith Jesus gave them leave. And the unclean spirits went out, and entered into the swine: and the herd ran violently down a steep place into the sea, (they were about two thousand;) and were choked in the sea. (Mark 5:9–13)

Two thousand spirits or souls in one body must make for very crowded conditions. However, if an evil spirit can enter another body, why would not any spirit be able to do likewise? Whether a spirit is considered to be a good one, a neutral one, or an evil one should not alter its ability to enter a body. That spirit would then have a chance to attain spiritual freedom once again. But if the Annunaki are successful in turning mankind into a biological robot, the ability to seek, study, and attain spiritual freedom will be lost.

Many books have been written about people who have retained some memory of one or even several of their past lives. Many other people claim to have such memories even though they have not gone public with that information. Hopefully, some part of the process that is required to attain spiritual freedom had been learned in their previous life.

I believe that "while he may be found" refers to while mankind still retains the mental ability to study and seek, i.e., before we are turned into biological robots. Once a person becomes a biological robot, their soul will be trapped in that body for thousands, perhaps hundreds of thousands, of years. We must not allow that to happen. The Isaiah verses just above also state that the wicked (that is you and I, my brothers and sisters) should change the way we think.

We humans definitely need to change the way we think. We have been deceived for far too long. We need to change the way we think about God, about religion, about government, about our money system, and about ourselves just for starters. Then, we can begin to change the way we think about other people, about wars, about life, about death, about honesty, and about spiritual freedom. We also need to change the way we think about prayer.

I believe that prayer is very important; it is important because it causes one to think. If one is sincere about praying, one must think about what they are praying. I do not think that it necessarily matters whether you are praying to God or not. Again, he is quite sufficient without your prayers. One need not be praying to anyone or anything. Just pray; it makes you think.

I do not believe that just reading or reciting some prayer that someone else has written is particularly useful. All the rituals, ceremonial prayers, incantations, and such that are performed by our churches, synagogues, and mosques are of little value. Those require little or no thought. Muslims perform these kinds of incantations five times a day; what good has it done them? They still believe that they should kill the infidels, they believe in Jihad, and they continue to kill humans at an alarming rate. The Jews perform all kinds of ceremonial prayers that are supposed to commemorate the sacrifices of Old Testament times. They perform these types of prayers while banging their heads against the Wailing Wall and during their feasts. Well, maybe they do not actually bang their head against the wall, but you know what I mean. What good has it done them? They continue to kill the descendents of Ishmael at an alarming rate. Christians perform many such prayers during our services, during mass, etc., and in all kinds of places. What good has it done us? We continue to have military personnel all over the world. We act as though we are supposed to police the entire Earth. We continue to kill other humans at an alarming rate. Prayer should be honest and sincere and make one think and should not be ritualistic.

Why do you think the Annunaki, through Jesus, told us the following in Matthew 6:9–13:

> After this manner therefore pray ye: Our Father which art in heaven, Hallowed be thy name. Thy kingdom come. Thy will be done in earth, as it is in heaven. Give us this day our daily bread. And forgive us our debts, as we forgive our debtors. And lead us not into temptation, but deliver us from evil: For thine is the kingdom, and the power, and the glory, for ever. Amen.

First, the Annunaki said, pray like this. God has never told anyone how to pray. The Annunaki knew that mankind would recite this prayer over and over ad infinitum without thinking; dumbing down continues. Our Father which art in heaven (the sky) are the Annunaki, not God. God is everywhere. Daily bread and debt are subtle ways to brainwash us and keep us in servitude. I want much more than daily bread; none of us should be in debt. We should not allow the Annunaki to keep us enslaved. We will not be in debt if we ever wake up and get rid of the Federal Reserve banking system. We can become much more than slaves if the Grandest Rebellion is successful. We must change the way we think.

The Annunaki have done a fantastic job of dumbing down humans, of keeping us in debt, and of making us work incessantly. What are our "works"? Our works are what we do. That includes the physical work we do; it includes what we do to make a living. It also includes our thinking and our decision making. If one has a thought or makes a decision, he has performed a work. James 2:14 asks this question:

> What doth it profit, my brethren, though a man say he hath faith, and have not works? can faith save him?

James says that man cannot attain spiritual freedom by faith alone. He then continues to say in James 2:17–20:

> Even so faith, if it hath not works, is dead, being alone. Yea, a man may say, Thou hast faith, and I have works: show me thy faith without thy works, and I will show thee my faith by my works. Thou believest that there is one God; thou doest well: the devils also believe, and tremble. But wilt thou know, O vain man, that faith without works is dead?

If one is going to attain spiritual freedom (salvation), one must work at it. It is not an easy task, and at this point in time, we do not know what must be learned in order to achieve the goal. Nevertheless, we are told to seek and told that we will find.

In order for one to seek, one must have the time to do so. The Annunaki have kept mankind so impoverished that many do not have the time to seek. Many have to work so hard just to make a living that there is no time to seek. We cannot all live in monasteries in order to have time to seek. We need to rethink some things.

I believe that it is good to work. I enjoy my work very much. However, it is more important to seek. Everyone should have time during their day to be still and quiet and seek. Our children should certainly be given time during their school day to be still and quiet and seek without being taught a bunch of false nonsense about who and what to seek.

In our world today, families that are composed of two parents residing together are fortunate. Far too many single-parent families exist. A single parent must find it extremely hard to find time to seek. Even when two parents remain together, far too many times, both parents have to work just to survive and provide for their children. That is a real shame and quite unnecessary. Too often, by the time these parents get home after work, they are too tired to do anything but turn on the TV and watch that nonsense. This causes them to be dumbed down even further. They have no time during their day to seek.

I will admit that we waste a lot of our time on things that are far less important than seeking. We attend all kinds of events that are entertaining but not very worthwhile. Some leisure and entertainment is good, but we do not seem to balance those things very well with studying and seeking. It really does not matter who wins the Super Bowl, the World Series, or any other game. We really have our priorities messed up when we pay millions of dollars to people who play those games and pay so little to the people who teach our children. We will spend over a billion dollars to build a stadium in which to play those games (sorry, Jerry Jones) while many of our children attend overcrowded classrooms in run-down neighborhoods and are being taught by inadequate teachers. We need to change the way we think.

Chapter 8

THINK

A year or two ago I read an absolutely fantastic novel entitled *Breakfast with Buddha*. It was written by Roland Merullo. I would highly recommend this book to any interested reader. The novel was fiction, was very well written, and was hilariously funny. I enjoyed many good laughs while reading the book; toward the end of the book, I also cried a little because there was a character in the book named Cecelia who reminded me of my youngest sister. Mr. Merullo used an analogy in the book that I hope he will not mind me using.

The analogy concerned our brain and our thinking. Two glasses of water were placed on a table. The water in each was crystal clear, and the water in each glass represented a human brain. Some dirt was placed into one of the glasses and the water was stirred. The water in that glass became quite murky and cloudy. That brain could not think clearly due to the murkiness of the water. As the dirt settled to the bottom of the glass that brain could think; however, it could not think as clearly as the one that was crystal clear. There are many things that cause our brains to become murky so that we do not think clearly.

Perhaps the main reason that we do not think clearly is because of the deception and confusion that the Annunaki have put into our brain. However, we cannot blame the Annunaki for all our shortcomings. We put a lot of dirt into our glass of water. I sincerely believe that being dishonest is one way that our glass becomes murky.

I suspect that all of us have known people who have become so entangled by their dishonesty that they do not even realize what the truth is. One lie leads to another; eventually, it becomes impossible to remember all the lies. I have had many patients during my medical career who have had that problem; I still have some.

I must admit that I do not understand why a person would be dishonest with their doctor. The information is protected by the doctor-patient relationship. The doctor is prohibited from disclosing that information to another person or entity. The dishonesty also severely restricts the doctor's ability to help the patient.

Television has been used by the Annunaki with great success in this regard. All the nonsense that appears on TV these days greatly muddies up our glass of water. One can hardly find any time, day or night, that some televangelist is not on TV spouting one false doctrine or another in their attempt to raise money. Television programming is such a mess that your glass is going to become very cloudy if you watch much television.

I must admit that there is one televangelist that I have some hope for. His name is Grant R. Jeffrey. He seems to be honest and sincere. He was raised in a Christian family and has a deep-seated faith in the Jesus deception. However, he has also done some serious work and some serious research. He has written a book entitled *Shadow Government*. If you can read this book without getting tangled up in the Jesus deception and the misdirected biblical prophecy stuff, it is a worthwhile read. Mr. Jeffrey has done a good job of researching and describing the international surveillance system known as Echelon. This international surveillance system is used by the Annunaki to gather as much information as possible on each of us. The book contains several other worthwhile topics as well. Mr. Jeffrey could become a tremendous ally in the Grandest Rebellion if we can overcome his deception about Jesus, God, and the Bible. If he is open-minded enough to study the ancient tablets from which the Bible was written, I believe that he might agree with me.

Pornography has become a multibillion-dollar industry in our world today. There are many muddy glasses of water in our world today as a result of our obsession with sex. Sex is a good thing. Obsession with it is not. I am far from a prudish person. As a young man, I engaged in many activities of which I am not proud. Moderation in all things is truly a virtue. One needs to find a balance in their lives in order to maintain crystal clarity in their glass of water and in their thinking. If one spends too much time dwelling on sex, food, alcohol, drugs, or anything else, it muddies their water. One can even spend too much time dwelling on prayer and meditation; one can spend too much time seeking. Few have that problem; however, there are some who spend so much time trying to become heavenly that they are no earthly good.

I can clearly recall a time during my childhood when my glass of water was almost completely clear. That was probably around sixty-five years ago. My glass of water had not become muddied with the things of the world. During those years, while asleep, I would oftentimes have dreams. During those dreams, there were many times that I would dream that I was flying around my neighborhood, observing things from the air that were occurring on the ground. At that time, I had never been in an airplane. Nevertheless, I realize today that my aerial perspective was quite accurate.

I have not thought about those dreams very much over the years until I began writing this book. Today, I believe that those dreams were actually out-of-body experiences. They were very enjoyable and quite exciting. During those dreams, even at that young age, I must have had some dirt in my glass because there were times that I had to struggle to get high enough to fly over telephone lines, electrical lines, and such. If you think back on your childhood, my guess is that you have had out-of-body experiences as well. I believe that each of us could enjoy such experiences on a regular basis if we could get our glass of water clear enough.

Our emotions can certainly cloud our thinking. If our emotions get out of balance, our thinking also gets out of balance. For instance, if we get too angry, too happy, too hungry, too thirsty, too tired, too sad, or if any emotion becomes too excessive, we will not think as clearly as we could. The brain is an amazing instrument. I believe that we would all be shocked if we could get our glass of water clear enough to experience what our mind can do for us.

I have found that my glass of water is slowly clearing. It is clearing because I have made an honest effort to put crystal clear water into my glass. I have also tried to not allow any dirt to enter my glass. My hope is that I can get my glass of water as clear as it was as a child.

If you decide to join us in the Grandest Rebellion, your glass needs to become crystal clear as well. I hope that we will attract many who will begin to make a real effort to clear their glass. We will need very clear thinking in order to alter the fate of mankind.

Chapter 9

THE TWO-EDGED SWORD

In the first chapter of the Revelation to John in verses 12–16 we find the following:

> And I turned to see the voice that spake with me. And being turned I saw seven golden candlesticks; And in the midst of the seven candlesticks one like unto the Son of man, clothed with a garment down to the foot, and girt about the paps with a golden girdle. His head and his hairs were white like wool, as white as snow; and his eyes were as a flame of fire; And his feet like unto fine brass, as if they burned in a furnace; and his voice as the sound of many waters. And he had in his right hand seven stars: and out of his mouth went a

sharp twoedged sword: and his countenance was
as the sun shineth in his strength.

In the second chapter of the Revelation in verse 12 we
find the following:

And to the angel of the church in Pergamos
write; These things saith he which hath the sharp
sword with two edges.

And in the fourth chapter of Hebrews in verse 12 we
find the following:

For the word of God is quick, and powerful,
and sharper than any two-edged sword, piercing
even to the dividing asunder of soul and spirit,
and of the joints and marrow, and is a discerner
of the thoughts and intents of the heart.

The words that have come out of the mouth of Jesus are,
indeed, sharper than a two-edged sword and are definitely
a discerner of our thoughts and of our intentions. His
words almost always have a double meaning. His words may
have an element of truth in them; however, there is almost
always an element of deception as well. By the time that
he began his public ministry, he had been brainwashed
by the Annunaki. By that time he was committed to help

them further their agenda. His words contain some truth, but they are rarely the whole truth and nothing but the truth. I will give you some examples.

Let us look carefully at some of the things that he said during one of his famous performances that is now called the Sermon on the Mount. This sermon is found at the beginning of the fifth chapter of Matthew. Beginning in verse 3, he says,

> Blessed are the poor in spirit: for theirs is the kingdom of heaven.

The humans who become poor in spirit are the biological robots who have had their spirit crushed. They do get to live with the Annunaki in New Jerusalem as slaves. Therefore, they have inherited the kingdom of heaven. These words of Jesus are the truth, but they are far from the whole truth and nothing but the truth. They are a two-edged sword.

In verse 4, Jesus says,

> Blessed are they that mourn: for they shall be comforted.

Big deal; who wants to mourn? This verse is simply a subliminal suggestion that mankind should accept the unremitting physical hardships and sacrifices that the

Annunaki have forced upon us. The ones who mourn may be comforted by other humans; they will not be comforted by the Annunaki.

In verse 5, Jesus says,

> Blessed are the meek: for they shall inherit the
> earth.

This is really cruel. If you are meek and just accept what the Annunaki are going to do to you, you will inherit the earth. The earth that you will inherit is the ground under which you are buried.

In verse 6, Jesus says,

> Blessed are they which do hunger and thirst
> after righteousness: for they shall be filled.

Seeking righteousness is a good thing; members of all religions must be seeking righteousness. They have indeed been filled with all kinds of deception.

In verse 7, Jesus says,

> Blessed are the merciful: for they shall obtain
> mercy.

This is a true statement; however, the mercy that one will obtain does not come from Jesus or the Annunaki.

The mercy that one will obtain by being merciful to other humans also comes from other humans.

In verse 8, Jesus says,

> Blessed are the pure in heart: for they shall see God.

Where is the blessing? Revelation 1:7 says,

> Behold, he cometh with clouds; and every eye shall see him, and they also which pierced him: and all kindreds of the earth shall wail because of him. Even so, Amen.

Like I said, where is the blessing? Every eye shall see him whether pure in heart or not. This verse refers to the next coming of Nibiru (God). When Nibiru rises in our skies, it will be seen in Israel (which pierced him). The kindreds (the Establishment) will indeed wail when they realize they have been so terribly deceived by the Annunaki and by Jesus.

In verse 9, Jesus says,

> Blessed are the peacemakers: for they shall be called the children of God.

Again, I ask, where is the blessing? Being called a child of the Annunaki is of no value.

In verse 10, Jesus says,

> Blessed are they which are persecuted for
> righteousness' sake: for theirs is the kingdom of
> heaven.

My belief is that this verse says that the Annunaki who
have been killed while supporting Enlil in the family feud
will be resurrected and live in New Jerusalem.

But that is enough of the Sermon on the Mount. I
think that you see the two-edged nature of the words of
Jesus. There is some truth there, but it is certainly not the
whole truth and nothing but the truth. We find similar
forms of deception about Jesus throughout the Bible.
For instance, Jesus is repetitively called both the Son of
God and the Son of man in the Bible. He is the son of
the god of the Bible (Enlil). He is also the Son of man,
i.e., the son of Mary. The deception, or the whole truth,
is almost never revealed in the Bible. Nevertheless, there
are occasions when Jesus does speak the whole truth.

An example of Jesus speaking the whole truth can be
found in Matthew 10:34–36:

> Think not that I am come to send peace on earth:
> I came not to send peace, but a sword. For I am
> come to set a man at variance against his father,
> and the daughter against her mother, and the

daughter-in-law against her mother-in-law. And a man's foes shall be they of his own household.

How true! How true! There may still be some out there who believe a Supreme Being (God) would do such a thing, but I surely do not understand how anyone could believe so.

I would like to make a point about another statement that Jesus made. He said in Matthew 26:11:

For ye have the poor always with you; but me ye have not always.

Again in Mark 14:7 he says,

For ye have the poor with you always, and whensoever ye will ye may do them good: but me ye have not always.

And in John 12:8, he repeats,

For the poor always ye have with you; but me ye have not always.

Jesus wanted to make sure that our thinking remained very cloudy. Poor thinking ensures that some will always remain poor. We have had poor people ever since the Adam was created. As long as the influence of the Annunaki is prevalent in our lives, some will remain poor. There will always be certain people who have the ability to make more money than others and who have the ability to obtain most of the money that others earn if that is their desire. However, this condition can be changed.

I believe that mankind has the ability to seek more lofty goals than those of the Annunaki. The goal of the Annunaki is to obtain all the gold and wealth in the world. Our goal should be to obtain spiritual freedom. All humans would then have almost equal abilities. The ability to attain spiritual freedom is not necessarily enhanced by intelligence, knowledge concerning the business world, or the other advantages that some enjoy when obtaining wealth is the goal. One may enjoy huge advantages in obtaining wealth if they have the ability to be dishonest, conniving, or ruthless. A lack of concern for the welfare of others is also helpful. Those advantages are lost, and actually become a hindrance, when the goal is to attain spiritual freedom.

Our little planet contains enough for everyone. The Annunaki may have taken most of the gold, silver, and other precious metals. Those things are not very important when the goal is obtaining spiritual freedom. We can easily grow enough food to feed everyone. We have enough resources to shelter everyone; some homes may have to be made out of mud bricks using slime for mortar (like the Tower of Babel), but we can all live quite comfortably. There is absolutely no reason that mankind should have poor among us. We must rid ourselves from the influence of the double-edged sword, clear our water glasses, and seek more lofty goals than those of the Annunaki.

I actually feel sorry for Jesus. He is such a tragic figure in all this. What he becomes is not his fault; he was simply the person who was produced when Mary was artificially inseminated with the sperm of Enlil. He began to be brainwashed at a very young age; he really had no chance to escape the clutches of Enlil. Shortly after being resurrected, he was whisked off to Nibiru. I am sure that Enlil has continued to stir Jesus's water glass vigorously to keep his thinking quite muddled. Jesus will then be unleashed upon mankind to do the dirty work for Enlil when the time is right. For his sake, as well as ours, we should make every effort to alter the fate of mankind.

I will provide a way for you to contact me; I invite you to do so. I hope that everyone who reads this book will join me in the Grandest Rebellion. However, before you contact me, be sure that your water glass is quite clear, be sure that you are 100 percent convinced that you understand the truth about the Bible, and be sure that you are willing to take the risks that will be involved in joining the rebellion.

Confession

They say that confession is good for the soul. I would like to confess to the readers of this book that I am not smart enough or clever enough to have reached the conclusions that I have come to in this book from my own studies. When the truth about the Annunaki is eventually revealed to mankind at some time in the future, I want everyone to know that I am not a prophet. God did not tell me to write this book. I assure you that the devil didn't either. However, as I wrote the book, I do feel that some power that is far greater than me put thoughts and ideas into my mind that I had never had before. I am simply a dumbed-down slave who may have had his brain cut in half. Perhaps it is just time for the Annunaki to be exposed for what they are and for the Bible to be exposed for what it is: a masterpiece of revelation and a travesty of deception.

I realize that it appears as though I am criticizing preachers, priests, rabbis, theologians, and all religious teachers in this book. I would like to apologize to every one of you. My intent is not to be critical of you individually. I understand that you have been misled and deceived just like the rest of us. I do hope that some of you will read this book. I hope that some of you will give serious thought and additional study to some of the things that you are teaching after reading this book. My intent is simply to inform mankind about what I believe to be the truth. I hope that a lot of people will read this book. I hope that after reading this book, some of them will stop listening to and supporting the teachings that are now being taught by the religious teachers.

The Annunaki did not forewarn mankind about the flood. I cannot imagine the horror that the poor souls must have gone through who were present on Earth at the time of its occurrence. The Annunaki could have saved many more of them than they did. I do not know whether forewarning mankind about the next great natural disaster will be beneficial or not. Mankind will have at least been forewarned if this book is disseminated widely enough. My most sincere hope is that they can do something to survive it.

I should also state for the record that my love for the Bible and my study of it will not cease just because I have come to believe that it is a story about the Annunaki rather than one about God. I have said in my book that the Bible contains great truths. Much wisdom can be gained by studying the Bible. The Bible contains wonderful verses about loving our fellow man and great advice such as the Ten Commandments and Golden Rule. Very beautiful words are found in the Song of Songs or the thirteenth chapter of 1 Corinthians about love. Many verses can be found that benefit mankind. It is a masterpiece of revelation. The love for the Bible and study of it changed my life tremendously for the better. I believe that just like the good book says, "The truth will set you free."

I moved to a small rural area in southeast Texas in November of 1998. I opened a small medical clinic at that time. I have remained at that location and have continued to run the clinic ever since.

In 1999, I do not recall exactly when, I had an experience that I would like to share with you. At that time, I had never heard of Zecharia Sitchin or the Annunaki. I had a dream one night. In that dream, I was out of my body and in the spirit, as they say. I saw a music stand with sheet music on the stand. The music was open, and I was in the air above it. Then suddenly, I passed through the music. I immediately knew that I had been transported into another dimension; I was aware that the way that I had been able to get into that dimension had something to do with sound waves.

Upon arriving into that dimension, I remained in the air. I was looking down on a scene of a small clearing with trees at the edge of the clearing. There were some men standing near the trees at the edge of the clearing. They all had long beards and were dressed in long heavy robes; I thought that there were ten to twelve of them. A young child was running and playing in the clearing; the men were watching the child play. I was aware that I was the child; the child was naked and his skin was snow white. As the child came near the men, a message came into my mind. The message was IUADAMO. I have often thought about that dream and wondered what IUADAMO meant.

I do not know what any of that means, if anything. I would love to be able to ask Zecharia Sitchin whether those letters mean anything in the Sumerian language. The men who were watching me run around naked as a jaybird looked exactly like and were dressed exactly like some of the pictures of the Annunaki in the ancient tablets.

If anyone would like to contact me, they may do so by e-mail at drjack@cmaaccess.com.

CPSIA information can be obtained at www.ICGtesting.com
231132LV00007B/4/P